RETHINKING ISLAMISM

'Meghnad Desai has given us a much needed guide to the complex role of Islam in current geopolitical conflicts. Bringing together a wealth of historical knowledge with powerful insights into globalisation, he shows that Global Islam is a revolutionary movement in many ways like those of the twentieth century. This is a book that deserves to be very widely read.'

JOHN GRAY, Professor of European Thought
at the London School of Economics and author of
Al Qaeda and What It Means To Be Modern (Faber)

'Like Maynard Keynes, Meghnad Desai is so much more than an economist. He has something arresting and original to say on almost any subject, and in this book he has brilliantly turned his formidable mind and erudition to the most urgent issue of the contemporary world – one which we misjudge at our peril.'

ROBERT SKIDELSKY, Professor of Political Economy
at the University of Warwick and author of
The World After Communism: A Polemic for Our Times

RETHINKING ISLAMISM

The Ideology of the New Terror

MEGHNAD DESAI

I.B. TAURIS

LONDON · NEW YORK

Published in 2007 by
I.B.Tauris & Co. Ltd
6 Salem Rd, London W2 4BU
175 Fifth Avenue, New York NY 10010
www.ibtauris.com

In the United States and Canada distributed by Palgrave Macmillan,
a division of St. Martin's Press, 175 Fifth Avenue, New York, NY 10010

ISBN   978 1 84511 267 7

A full CIP record for this book is available from the British Library
A full CIP record for this book is available from the Library of Congress
Library of Congress catalog card: available

Typeset in Van Dijck by illuminati, Grosmont,
www.illuminatibooks.co.uk
Printed and bound in Great Britain by
T.J. International Ltd, Padstow, Cornwall

Contents

Preface

London experienced the new terrorism on 7 July 2005 when four bombs were detonated around the city. In the debate and discussion that followed I noticed that there was too much focus on Islam as a religion and on Muslims as a community, as if each deserved examination as a likely pathology which led to the bombs. I expressed my disagreement with such views in a letter that was published in the *Financial Times* on 10 August 2005. I argued there that what caused the terrorism was not Islam as a religion or even the lifestyle or culture of Muslims in Britain but an ideology, Global Islamism, whose nature had to be grasped if we were to fight terrorism. I drew an analogy between Soviet Communism and Global Islamism as ideologies which had an anti-Western agenda and asked whether we could combat one ideology as we did the other. The letter elicited a response by Martin Wolf in the *FT* as well as some correspondence. I was then approached by Alex Wright of I.B. Tauris and invited to submit a book proposal developing my argument.

This short book – really an extended essay – is the result. I examine the history of the Middle East over the last hundred years. I look at the nature of ideology in general, examining Marxism–Leninism, anarchism, Nazism and nationalism as likely analogues to Global Islamism. The core of the book is devoted to a careful study of Osama Bin Laden's speeches and fatwas. Whatever people may think of his terrorist activities, the ideology Bin Laden has fashioned, Global Islamism, remains a powerful force that will outlive him. Al-Qaeda is a threat not because it has training camps, finance and bombs, but because it is a brand for this ideology which, like a virus, can spread globally. In fighting terrorists we need intelligence, police and international cooperation. But in fighting terrorism, we need to grasp the nature of the ideology, which is easy to spread and difficult to counter. I devote therefore a chapter to the lessons we have learnt from fighting other ideologies that will be useful in countering Global Islamism.

The book was written substantially over the Christmas break in 2005. While I was reading the proofs, on 10 August 2006 (exactly a year after my *FT* letter), yet another case of an alleged terrorist plot to detonate bombs on planes was revealed. There was also a month-long war between Israel and Hezbollah on the Israel–Lebanon border, and between Israel and Hamas in the Gaza. I have done the necessary updating but kept it to a minimum, as my essay seemed to be just as relevant now. I trust readers will agree.

I am grateful to John Gray, Sayyed Nadeem Kazmi and Robert Skidelsky for reading the manuscript and saying supportive things. I am grateful to the librarians of the House of Lords library for obtaining books and documents. As always, Kishwar Desai was a source of help and inspiration. I thank them all.

September 2006

London, 7/7

'A bomb outrage to have any influence on public
opinion now must go beyond the intention of
vengeance or terrorism. It must be purely
destructive. It must be that, and only that,
beyond the faintest suspicion of any other object.'
(Vladimir the diplomat, speaking to Verloc the
anarchist, in Joseph Conrad, *The Secret Agent*)

Early one morning on a busy weekday, Thursday the 7th of July
2005, three bombs exploded on the London Underground, the city-
wide tube transport network, and an hour later a bomb blew up a
bus along with, most likely, the suspect bomber himself.

London had seen nothing like it since the Second World War.
It had faced the Blitz bravely and towards the end of the War
there were the German V2 bombers. But this was different. It was
sudden, though not unexpected. Police had been warning citizens
for a long time that some sort of attack was imminent, though
they had also promised they would do their best to stop it. All
the same, when it came, it was devastating. And yet there was not

much to see above the ground. The iconic image of 7/7 will always be the number 30 bus in Tavistock Square near Upper Woburn Place, standing still for hours like a piece of modernist sculpture, its top torn off and the rest of it twisted in an odd but horrifying yet fascinating misshape. That was the first and, for a while, the only visible sign. But slowly on television and radio, news trickled out. At 8.50 a.m. there had been three explosions within seconds of each other in the London Underground, and at 9.47 a.m. the bus blew up.

The injured and the dead were brought out. As many as 700 people were injured and at the final count 56 had died, including the four alleged suicide bombers. They were of all nationalities – from Sierra Leone, China, Israel, Poland, New Zealand, Colombia, South Africa, Australia, Ireland and of course the local British, who themselves are a global racial and ethnic cocktail. The first to come out were the bus victims. Then the passengers on the three underground trains. London's tube transport system is dug very deep below the surface since much of it it has to go below the River Thames, which winds across the city in a serpentine zigzag. There are twelve lines with their exotic names – Bakerloo, Jubilee, Hammersmith & City – with colour-coding for visitors unfamiliar with the names to find their way around using the tube map. The Circle Line is the most shallow as it does not cross the river. So the first bodies to be brought out were from one of the two Circle Line trains targeted. The train on which the bomb had been set off had been standing at the Edgware Road station platform. The other two trains were in-between stations, one again on the Circle Line going from Liverpool Street station to Aldgate in the East End of London, and the other deep underground on the Piccadilly Line, which runs across London from the north-east to the south-west, crossing the Thames. It is the deepest line. It was travelling from King's Cross to Russell Square, not that far from Tavistock Square where the bus later exploded. It took ages to reach it and free the bodies. The hot summer day, with the temperature reaching 60°C underground, the depth, the oxyacetylene torches needed to cut the metal – all added to the harshness of the task the rescuers faced. It was weeks before the line could resume operation.

Londoners coped. They were stoical. Within hours a website purporting to be al-Qaeda in Europe claimed 'Britain is now burning with fear, terror and panic in its northern, southern, eastern and western quarters.'

There was no panic, no fear that anyone saw. There was shock and much sorrow as people went about their daily tasks. Many stopped and helped with the rescue operation. Doctors and medical staff in the British Medical Association's offices near Tavistock Square were quick to help the bus victims. Slowly the dead and injured were brought to the surface and moved to hospitals. The dead numbered 56, including four of the (alleged) bombers; 700 were injured, some seriously. They were an eclectic mix of nationalities, religions, colours, ages. London is indeed a global village, a tossed salad of diverse diasporas.

Parliament met, since it was a scheduled day for it to meet. A statement was read out by the Home Secretary, Charles Clarke, in the House of Commons. As is the practice, it was repeated word for word in the House of Lords by the Deputy Leader, Lord Rooker. I heard it; I was there. I had left home in Denmark Hill in South-east London upon getting a phone call from my sister in Mumbai, who had seen a television report about London bombs. We had not even switched the television on. It was, after all, too early in the day to be watching television (since then we have switched it on first thing every morning). I left quickly and got to Westminster. No hitch, no problem – not south of the river, nor north of the river. The statement was calmly received. There was already an urge not to demonise any community. Stay calm and don't lose your head, was the message. The fight against terrorism will be a long one and patience is required if we are to win it.

First comes the shock and then the grief. Anger soon follows and questions are asked. How can it happen here? Who had done this? We found out that there were four young men whose images were caught on CCTV. It could never be proved but the implication is that they most likely were the suicide bombers. Who were they? The four alleged bombers were, as far as we can tell, British-born and -bred young men, their ages ranging from 18 to 30. They were Hasib Hussain (18), Mohammad Sidique Khan (30), Shehzad Tanwir (22), all from Leeds and all from families that had originally come from Pakistan, and Jamal (Germaine) Lindsay from Luton (age uncertain), whose family had Jamaican connections.

They were all Muslims. How could British-born young men become suicide bombers? people asked. Why would they do it? Was it alienation? people inquired, using that fashionable but vague word. Were they unhappy, discriminated against, poor? Is it something to do with Islam? Are Muslims, as a rule, given to bombing?

These questions hung in the air for a long time. Many newspapers had column yards, not just inches, devoted to them. Islam was dissected, British policy in Iraq and Afghanistan castigated, police blamed for missing the signals of an imminent attack. By the time another attack took place on 21/7, it was like déjà vu. The police blundered in, shooting dead a young Brazilian man, suspecting him to be a suicide bomber. Mistaken identity. They all look alike. Who are they? Are we all them?

Yet we have to understand why such tragedies happen and why they will recur. At least for a while until we understand and tackle the root cause. There should be no surprise that the alleged bombers were British-born. Why should there be? In Northern Ireland, British-born Catholic and Protestant young men and women have been detonating bombs at home and on the mainland for some time now. Yet we don't question whether Christians are as a rule bomb-throwers as a result of that experience. We know – perhaps some of us only vaguely – that the quarrel is about nationalism, about who belongs to which nation – the Irish Republic or the United Kingdom. It is not about religion; it is not the theological dispute between Protestants and Catholics which Martin Luther ignited, and the answer is not for all of us to go and read the Bible, to study Christianity and sympathise with the Christians in their peculiar desire to destroy their own neighbourhoods.

So why do we think Islam is the problem? Why do we rush to the Qur'an and listen to the mullahs? Why don't we think that, like many other quarrels around the world, the root cause is political, not theological? The Reverend Dr Ian Paisley, leader of the Democratic Unionist Party in Northern Ireland, has been staunchly against any compromise with the IRA, and he has written many books on Protestant theology. But we don't read his books to grasp the nettle of the Ulster question. Why, then, don't we treat the suicide bombers the same as other political malcontents?

One of the alleged bombers was shown on an al-Qaeda video released in September 2005. Mohammad Sidique Khan was heard saying:

> Your democratically elected governments continuously perpetuate atrocities against my people all over the world. And your support of them makes you directly responsible, just as I am directly responsible for protecting and avenging my Muslim brothers and sisters. Until we feel security you will be our targets and until you stop the bombing, gassing, imprisonment and torture of my people we will not stop this fight. We are at war and I am a soldier. Now you too will taste the reality of this situation.

This statement is one of the many issued by al-Qaeda to construct a duality in the world today. It sets up a conflict between the governments of the West and their citizens, on the one hand, and Muslims worldwide, on the other. Soon after the end of the Cold War in the early 1990s, Samuel Huntington, a Harvard professor, wrote an article titled 'The Coming Clash of Civilizations?', predicting in an uncanny way the scenario painted in Mohammad Sidique Khan's statement. He subsequently published a book with the term 'Clash' again in the title. At the time of the publication of the article and then the book, many reviewers and fellow academics of Huntingdon took the view that he had exaggerated the threat or simplified too much in creating the notion of two civilisations.[1] There were, they argued, no such simple wholes as the West and the Islamic Civilization. Fred Halliday, professor of International Relations at the LSE and an expert on the Middle East, takes a view which is close to the one taken here. We need to demarcate between Islam as a religion and the political use of the religion which is labelled Islamism.

Yet there is something after all, whatever one calls it, which has to be recognised in Huntington's argument of confrontation. Al-Qaeda has decidedly adopted a Huntingtonian view of the nature of the conflict, as Mohammad Sidique Khan's statement shows. Indeed, as we shall see further below, Osama Bin Laden's view is also of a clash between two 'wholes' – the Crusader West and the Muslim community, the *umma*. So it would appear as if Huntington's 'reductionist' entities (as his Harvard colleague, Nobel prize-winning economist Amartya Sen, has called them) have been fused with reality by Osama Bin Laden. What is more, the idea of such a confrontation is taking on an increasingly sinister reality.

As if to buttress this sinister reality, later in that month of September 2005, a small event occurred which passed unnoticed almost all over the world. An author in Denmark wrote a book for Danish children on the life of Prophet Muhammad. But he found that no one would illustrate for him a likeness of the Prophet. Flemming Rose, the arts editor for the Danish newspaper *Jyllands Posten* heard of this and commissioned twelve cartoons of the Prophet. They were not works of art by any account; some were scurrilous – one with Muhammad's turban shaped like a bomb, one with him apologising to a newly dead suicide bomber that he had run out of the virgins God had promised. The rest were, from what we gather, not very amusing. (The British press chose not to reproduce any of the cartoons. The BBC displayed one of them on its news programme, which had been reprinted in *France-Soir.*)

The cartoons were reproduced in an Egyptian newspaper *Al-Agar* soon after, and there was no reaction. A group of Danish imams protested and asked for a meeting with the Danish prime minister, Anders Fogh Rasmussen. He took the view that what a newspaper did was not his business. The freedom of the press in Denmark meant that newspapers were beyond the control of government. Some imams in Denmark then took their campaign to condemn the Danish government to Saudi Arabia and Egypt. But they took as their evidence not just the 12 published cartoons but three more, including one with the Prophet as a paedophile and one with a pig snout. (This was reported in a Danish tabloid *Extra Bladet* and not denied.)

What followed was predictable. In the Middle Eastern countries, a protest arose regarding this insult to Islam. The editor of *Jyllands Posten*, Carsten Juste, refused to apologise. The Danish prime minister insisted he could not censure the newspaper. Then a Norwegian Christian weekly, *Magasinet*, reprinted the cartoons. Things began to get worse. By 30 January 2006, when Danish business was facing a boycott across the Muslim countries, Rasmussen admitted that things had gone too far and apologised. This inflamed some European newspapers that wished to assert the freedom of the press. *Die Welt* in Germany duly republished the cartoons, as did French, Spanish, Italian and Dutch newspapers. This outraged Muslim sentiments further. Danish and Norwegian embassies in the Middle East came under attack, and one in Damascus was burned down.

The Muslim world was still divided. A Jordanian weekly, *Shihan*, reprinted the cartoons on 2 February to argue that Islam was insulted more by the public beheading of hostages seen on television performed by Islamic terrorist groups than by such cartoons. The editors Jihad al-Momini and Hashim al-Khalidi were sacked and soon faced prosecution. Mr Momini suffered a heart attack and was taken to hospital. In London, there were demonstrations on 3

February by Muslims; some carried placards promising a return of
7/7 as a deserved punishment for the cartoons. Posters asked for
the beheading of anyone connected with such publications. Muslims were said to be incensed at this insult to Islam. The display
of posters urging beheadings and assassinations, praising the 7/7
bombers, caused a counter-outrage from relatives of the victims
of the 7 July bombings. Soon moderate Muslim opinion was dis-
owning the demonstrators and held a counter-demonstration on
Saturday 11 February and on the following Saturday to insist that
Islam was a peaceable religion.

The concentrated, perhaps even orchestrated, fury against Denmark and Norway was something of a surprise. It is America and
its faithful ally Britain that have attracted most of the hostility
from Muslims in recent years. This is partly because of Britain's
role as an empire in the break-up of the Ottoman Empire after
the First World War and America's support for Israel over the last
several decades. The war in Afghanistan in 2001 and later Iraq
in 2003 and since have added to that resentment. The rest of the
European Union, on the other hand, has escaped such fury. The
Scandinavian countries have on the whole been exemplary in their
international behaviour throughout the post-war period. They
have avoided any military involvement, been prominent in giving
overseas development assistance, and, in the case of Norway, been
helpful in mediating in international disputes, most notably in the
Oslo Accords between Israel and the Palestine Liberation Organisation. The spread of the Muslim fury to Scandinavia has polarised
opinion in the Western countries. There is a lot of criticism of
America and Britain, both at home in the two countries and all
over Europe. Some people even take the view that America has

brought the al-Qaeda attacks upon itself. Yet the Muslim fury against Denmark and Norway looks like an overreaction. What is at issue?

Now there is a puzzle here. There is no Qur'anic injunction against portraying the Prophet. Islam shares with the other two monotheisms of the Middle East the ban on idol worship, since God presumably is not representable in any human image. But so far as the Prophet is concerned, there were coins struck with his image soon after his death, as early as the seventh century CE.[2] There was a long-standing tradition of depiction of the Prophet which survives in manuscripts as late as the fifteenth century at least, so Stephen Bates argued in his *Guardian* column on 2 February 2006. Among the Shi'a there is no ban on pictures of the Prophet. Thus the ban on pictures of the Prophet is a recent development, though it is not clear when it became absolute, if it ever did. There is only one sentence in a Hadith (traditions of what the Prophet said during his lifetime), declaring that the angels do not enter a house where there are animals or images. There is no further elaboration of why images are so unwelcome to the angels.

The genuine strong feeling of outrage among Muslims is obviously partly because, whatever the history of the ban, many believe it is decreed by high authorities, perhaps the Prophet himself. The depiction of the Prophet with a turban shaped like a bomb also conflated him with terrorists. But the slow reaction to the publication in September, the agitation by the imams in Denmark to rope in Saudi Arabia and Egypt, the official support for the burning of embassies in Syria and for the riots in other Middle Eastern countries, lead to the conclusion that what is at stake here is not religion but politics.

Religions are, at one level, systems of belief about the here and now, and about what happens in the afterlife. But as they affect societies, they become a powerful force in their own right. The separation of religion and public political life is a very recent, and indeed fragile, achievement of Western liberal societies. Yet it cannot be presumed to be universal. It is certainly not so in many non-Western countries. While in the West, religion is supposed to be part of the private lives of individuals and kept out of public political life, other countries are wedded to politics being ruled by religion and governments enforcing a religious code. There is thus at the very least a conflict, if not a clash, between two world-views. Globalisation has ended the relative isolation in which such conflicting views coexisted. We need therefore to examine the interrelationship between religion and politics carefully.

Islam is a peaceful religion like all other religions. But every religion – Islam, Judaism, Christianity, Hinduism, and even Buddhism – has been used to incite warlike feelings. When in power, backed by armies, every religion can inspire killings. The church of every warring nation in the two world wars blessed the combatants and told them to annihilate the enemy, and assured them that 'their' god was with them. In the 1950s in the USA there used to be a slogan, 'Kill a Commie for Christ', and it was not entirely facetious. It was only in the late twentieth century that many Christian churches became pacifist and tolerant. The memory of Christian anti-Semitism is recent for any reader of twentieth-century history and even some filmgoers, as the con-troversy over Mel Gibson's film *The Passion* showed. Religion can be used to violent purposes as well as peaceful ones. It is not the religion, it is how it is put to use politically, that determines such matters. We need to rethink religion politically and not just treat it as religion. If we don't, then there will be something missing from our capacity to cope with the political consequences of religious beliefs. In the recent terrorist attacks, it is religion as a political force that is uppermost. We ignore this at our peril.

This book – an extended essay – is designed to fill that lacuna. It takes the view that what we face in the recent upsurge in terrorism is not a religion but an ideology. That ideology wears religious garb, but we have to see through that garb and discern the political lineaments beneath. The ideology is Global Islamism. It is the ideology of global terrorism. No matter how evil it may be, we have to learn that it has a coherent story to tell which has inspired thousands of Muslims, and made them take absurd risks even to the act of suicide bombing. Anything that has that much influence has to be taken seriously, and understood, if we are to fight it. Fight it we must because it is an ideology which is not amenable to debate or dialogue. It does not indulge in multi-faith conversations or ecumenical congresses. It believes that its goal requires terror and unrelenting terror until its ends are achieved. Fighting terrorists, preventing them from doing harm, tracking down their cells, stopping their financial sources are things the police and the intelligence services can do best. But fighting terrorism is about fighting an ideology. Only ideas can defeat ideas, not guns.

So it is Global Islamism that we need to grasp. Yet it is an ideology like many that have previously influenced the world and often visited mayhem upon it. Global Islamism is like any other ideology in many ways, but at the same time it is different. What follows is an attempt to explain its nature, understanding it in its own terms and placing it in the wider context of the politics of ideologies.

ONE

Introduction

'The attack must have all the shocking senselessness
of gratuitous blasphemy.'
(Vladimir the diplomat, in
Joseph Conrad, *The Secret Agent*)

The Berlin Wall and the Twin Towers

Two dramatic events of the last twenty years share a pair of iconic
numbers. On 9/11, the World Trade Center towers were rammed
by planes hijacked by terrorists. On 11/9, a dozen years previously,
the Berlin Wall faced a different kind of assault.

The Berlin Wall did not fall; it was destroyed physically by the
bare hands of angry people from both sides of divided Germany
separated by the ugly structure, using very crude equipment. It
signalled the collapse of the last empire of the twentieth century
– the Communist empire centred in Russia. It was an empire that
was born in idealism, the dream of an equal society of Communism.
The tsar's government was tottering from the dismal performance

of Russian soldiers in the First World War, and early in 1917 the tsar abdicated. A spontaneous revolution elected soviets from around the country, which sat in parallel with the the Duma – the parliament pursuing the war in a divided and bitter country. The Bolsheviks were the most reviled revolutionaries in the soviets but steadily their slogan of 'Peace, Land and Bread' appealed to the millions of peasants who had gone to the front to fight as soldiers. On 25 October 1917 (according to the old-style calendar; 7 November in the new) the Bolsheviks won a majority in the Petrograd Soviet and grabbed power.

The October Revolution of 1917 was followed by a civil war, but the Bolsheviks held on to power.[3] Soon they consolidated and extended the tsar's empire into what became the Union of Soviet Socialist Republics (USSR), or the Soviet Union for short. After the defeat of Nazism in 1945, the Soviet Union extended its reaches into Eastern Europe. Its revolutionary message appealed to China, and Mao led the Chinese Communist Party to victory in 1949. Communism spread to Vietnam, Cambodia, Cuba, Ethiopia. At one stage, say around 1960, Communism looked like the future of the world. The Soviet empire already ruled over the eastern half of Europe and its friends ruled the largest country in Asia.

The empire had its beginning in obscure meetings of Russian Communist exiles, educated members of a privileged elite who had all escaped the tsarist police. Their quarrels concerned the theory and practice of revolution, of how to overthrow the tsarist state, a pledge of no compromise with liberal democrats and to distrust, above all, fellow socialists of whatever colour.

From such obscure beginnings, and led by Lenin, a genius who single-mindedly focused on the goal he had set, the Bolsheviks triumphed in establishing the first empire built on an ideology, Marx-ism–Leninism. The ideology had its own roots in a philosophy whose simple message of the future to come was underpinned by a fiendishly difficult theory, that of Marx and Engels. The philosophy was universalistic, cosmopolitan, egalitarian and millenarian. It was turned in the hands of Josef Stalin, who succeeded Lenin to the leadership of the Bolsheviks, into one of the most murderous state terrorisms ever known to the human species. His methods were enthusiastically copied by other Communist leaders once they came into power. It was a tragedy. The victims who suffered in the name of an egalitarian, cosmopolitan philosophy run into mil-lions across Eastern Europe and Eurasian Russia, China, Korea, Cambodia, the Horn of Africa and Latin America.[4]

Despite this terrible record, the ideology still commands sup-port across many countries in the world, where citizens study its philosophy, political parties argue its merits and universities teach courses in its philosophical foundations. The murderous leaders of these countries even now have a following, are displayed on T-shirts or have their names bestowed on newborn babies. The central terror machine was silenced soon after 1956 when Nikita Khrushchev, who had inherited Stalin's post as general secretary of the Communist Party, told the world how cruel and arbitrary Stalin's rule had been and how many people had perished, most of them loyal citizens of the Soviet Union and a large proportion of them Bolsheviks. The destruction of the Berlin Wall signalled the end, in Europe at least, of that regime. In 1989 the Communist empire in Eastern Europe, and in 1991 the USSR itself, collapsed. It did so without a shot being fired by its enemies, without the awesome nuclear arsenal on both sides of the Cold War being alerted, let alone used. The nightmare scenario of the Cold War – the *Dr Strangelove* fantasy – did not realise itself.

Yet what followed was not eternal peace or even a New World Order, as was much prophesied by the victors of the Cold War. Within a decade of the Wall disappearing, there was new talk of Armageddon. The world faced a new threat, a new 'clash of civilisations', which was unique and even more dangerous. It was the new unknown, the new global fear. It was the threat of Islamic terrorism, the fear of al-Qaeda. The 9/11 attacks on the World Trade Center in New York and the Pentagon in Washington DC were an unpleasant opening of the new century.

The attack was well planned. It leveraged a simple technology, aircraft filled with fuel, into weapons of mass destruction by the combination of hijacking and the suicide bomb. It was obviously crafted by people with foresight and high educational qualifications – engineers, trained pilots, graduates of distinguished universities of international repute. It was also an attack which had pedigree. Through the 1990s, the name of al-Qaeda was broadcast throughout the world as the lead agency in terrorism. Soon after the 9/11 events, the terror spread to Bali, Delhi, Madrid, Sharm-el-Sheikh, London. A separate branch of al-Qaeda is waging a terror war in Iraq, and in November 2005 the terrorist bombing inspired by the Iraq insurgents spread to Amman in Jordan, targeting Muslims.

But even before the appearance of al-Qaeda, in 1979, there had been the Iranian Revolution, which overthrew the Shah of Iran, held American Embassy staff hostage and, ten years later, issued a fatwa announcing a sentence of death on Salman Rushdie, the Indian-born author of many novels but most particularly of *The*

Satanic Verses. It was an early warning that a new intolerance may come with religious sanction to all our shores.

Communist state terrorism had a face. It was Josef Stalin, who for the thirty years of his dictatorship inspired worshipful loyalty and proceeded to wage an unrelenting war against the citizens of the USSR. In other countries, the face was of Mao or Pol Pot or Kim Il-Sung. But it was always the face of the Supreme Leader. The new terror also has a face – Osama Bin Laden. He too has zealous champions and his face appears on T-shirts. He has spawned other faces, much as Stalin did: Ayman al-Zawahiri, Hambali and Abu Musab al-Zarkawi. The face of the Iranian Revolution was Ayatollah Ruholla Khomeini.

Terrorism as a systematic violent assault on innocent civilian populations (i.e. those uninvolved with or unable to affect the issue at dispute between the terrorists and their avowed enemy) is sadly neither unknown nor infrequent in modern times. State terrorism is older and more systematic and less criticised. It is terrorism by groups which are not in power – by non-governmental organisations, so to speak – which is the subject of most debate today. But even to understand this latest brand of violence, a historical perspective is useful.

When 9/11 occurred, there was a small amount of smugness among the British, who thought they had seen a lot of IRA terror on the UK mainland, not to mention in Northern Ireland itself. The IRA called its struggle one of national liberation and its goal was the eventual unification of the two parts of Ireland. The UK government saw it as terrorism. Yet the IRA received funds from many Americans and invitations to the White House by presidents of both major parties. The dispute is now almost settled. It was achieved partly by negotiation and partly by military confrontation. The Americans changed their stance on IRA only after 9/11. This in itself shows how contingent the notion of terrorism is. Yet the struggle began in the nineteenth century, taking a new phase during the First World War and the declaration of Irish independence in 1922. A vicious civil war broke out then, but Ireland was partitioned into Eire and the British province of Ulster.

There are even now struggles for 'national liberation', or 'civil wars' as one's view may be, being fought in Palestine/Israel, Sri Lanka, Chechnya, Kashmir, where again acts of terrorism are committed and meet with less moral revulsion (at least away from the immediate vicinity of where the acts take place) than the international acts of al-Qaeda. These national liberation struggles follow the tradition of the anti-colonial struggles that were fought in the French, British, Dutch, Portuguese and Belgian Empires. The leaders of such nationalist and anti-colonial struggles were honoured and became presidents and prime ministers of their independent nations. Kenyatta, Makarios, Sukarno, Mugabe, Aung San and others were terrorists at one stage and statesmen the next.

Is, then, the present terrorism the same as before? Will the war on terror being waged by Western and some Third World governments end in compromise and negotiations? Will we see President Osama Bin Laden being welcomed on red carpets ten or twenty years from now by a future president of the USA or the British prime minister?[5] Is al-Qaeda a liberation movement with legitimate complaints against the imperialist West as Bin Laden claims? Is the West not hypocritical in waging a violent military war, in Iraq for instance, on the pretext of fighting terrorism and committing acts which are similar to those committed by terrorists?

The Religion Detour

There is one distinguishing feature of the new wave of terrorism that has done more than anything else to muddy the debate about its nature. This is the religious rhetoric which has been at the heart of its propaganda. The new terrorism wears Islamic garments. Its perpetrators recite and quote the Holy Qur'an. Its young agents the suicide bombers, men in most instances, go to their deaths with the promise of a paradise with scores of virgins waiting for them. Samuel Huntington was much criticised when he warned about a clash of civilisations between the West and Islam. His liberal critics pointed out many flaws in the argument, in the simplicity of clubbing large areas of the world under a single religious label, Islam. Yet the blunt truth in his prophecy is being affirmed by the terrorists themselves. They see it as a battle − a jihad − against the Crusaders − the very terminology drawing attention to the medieval battles between Christians and Muslims for Jerusalem.[6]

The religious garb of the new terror has been its most confusing aspect. When 9/11 struck, both President Bush and Prime Minister Blair were quick to affirm their tolerance of Islam and their abhorrence of terror. Everywhere in the West, people began a programme to understand the nature of Islam. Muslim leaders were quick to teach their fellow non-Muslim citizens the peaceful nature of Islam, to tell them that the Holy Qur'an did not condone such violence, that jihad, far from being the word for a Holy War, was nothing but the quotidian struggle to lead the good life in accordance with the teachings of the holy book.

The Western world is liberal, tolerant and, by and large, not intensely religious. In the Protestant regions of Europe, people are agnostic, if not atheist. The Catholics are tolerant and can never be fundamentalist, as they believe in Papal authority rather than in the text of the Bible as the final arbiter. In the USA, the East Coast liberal tradition is tolerantly mild and ecumenical as between Judaism and Christianity. Politicians running for electoral office have to display their church-going habits, but intense religiosity has the smell of redneck intolerance of the interior, the South and the south-west. The religious are on the right wing of the Republican Party. They are often Christian fundamentalists.

But while the attitude of many Western liberals towards Christian fundamentalism is one of horror and dismissive contempt, they find themselves helpless against Muslim fundamentalism. The possibility that they may face an accusation of racism cripples their critical faculties. This has to do with the history of the Western societies in the last third of the twentieth century. To see how and why this is so requires some explanation.

The Growth of Western Tolerance

The first half of the twentieth century saw the Anglo-American liberal democracies engaged in a battle against the anti-democratic forces of Junker imperialism and then fascism. Of course, there was a contradiction in the stance of some of the Allies since they had empires in which democracy or freedom were denied to millions, and in the case of colonies (as opposed to white settlements) there was rampant racism. Still, on balance, the Second if not the First World War was fought against an inherently evil philosophy of fascism in its German, Japanese and Italian variants. There was some justification in the Allies claiming, as they did in the Atlantic

Charter that they were fighting the battle for the four freedoms. The battle won, the democracies fought to achieve full employment and mass prosperity while conducting a cold war against the Communist empire. The experience of the Holocaust taught the West the horrible costs of intolerance and anti-Semitism. What happened in Germany was the extreme end of a long history of Christian anti-Semitism which prevailed in the Allied countries right up to 1939 if not beyond. What is called Judeo-Christian culture was a deliberate construction out of this harsh lesson in the need to avoid intolerance. It is as well to remember this because it is easily forgotten how recent the habits of ecumenical tolerance are. Some of the Western democracies had their own anti-colonial struggles to deal with – France with Indochina and Algeria; Belgium in Congo; Britain in Kenya, Rhodesia and Malaya. But even as these battles had to be managed, the first 25 years after 1945 were a period of peace and prosperity at home – a golden age indeed.

It was as a notice of the impending end of the golden age that students and young people generally rose in revolt across the Western world in 1968. These student revolts had much to do with US war in Vietnam and had the tacit approval of, if not active encouragement from, the Communist empire. The events of the Prague Spring of 1968 encouraged the students defy both sides of the Cold War. The anti-war movement in the USA also merged with the civil rights struggle, which had been going on since the mid-1950s. A revulsion against Western governments, especially that of the USA, became widespread among the young, and it soon took the form of anti-capitalist terrorism. Groups such as the Weathermen in the USA, Baader-Meinhof in Germany, the Angry Brigade in Britain and the Red Brigades in Italy were anti-establishment, anti-capitalist and anti-American. They were individualistic, anarchist and mindlessly violent. Their organisation anticipated later terrorist groups.

Even as these groups were successfully contained, the challenge of accommodating multiracial groups of immigrants from the ex-colonies began for many European countries. For the USA, the civil rights struggle continued, with the need to adapt social and political practice so as to reflect a culture of equality between the different racial groups. Immigrants were not new for America. Its problem was to give equal treatment to one of its oldest immigrant groups, the black population which had arrived as slaves from Africa in the eighteenth and nineteenth centuries. The efforts to build an anti-racist culture required meticulous knowledge of, and genuine respect for, the living practices and beliefs of the incoming groups. Political correctness required an immediate and unfailing respect for what may appear to be the strange practices of newcomers who were now citizens. When it came to the religious beliefs of the new citizens, even the most agnostic of Western liberals became willing, if not enthusiastic, sympathisers. All across primary and secondary schools in Britain, parents learnt about Diwali and Ramadan. School assemblies became multi-faith events, and the politically correct even frowned at celebrating Christmas too aggressively lest it offend the sentiments of the new citizens.

It was this background of newly learnt tolerance which made the debate about the new terrorism so difficult. How much was the new terrorism embedded in and 'natural' to the religion professed by the terrorists? What was the nature of Islam? Was it true that some of the preachers in the mosques so recently built were teaching hatred of the West and inciting young Muslims? Should we be tolerant of Islamic fundamentalism and accommodate it along with Christian fundamentalism, Jewish fundamentalism and the newfangled Hindu fundamentalism which had made its appearance on the Indian subcontinent in the 1990s?

Or was there a distinction to be made between moderate and extremist Muslims? Some liberals asked whether there was a problem with Islam itself. Was Islam by its nature intolerant of other religions, especially Judaism? Was the problem that Islam had not had a Reformation as Christianity had? Why was there no secular tradition in Muslim societies? Where were the young Muslim sceptics and atheists?[7]

Islam or Islamism?

There is much for all of us to learn about Islam and no doubt about Muslim culture and societies. But my argument in this book is that one needs above all to separate Islam as a religion in both theory and practice and *Islamism* as an ideology. It is the ideology which feeds terrorism. It puts on religious garb and takes shelter in quotations from the Qur'an. But the ideology is political, its aim being the winning of power over people. In this, Islamism is much like other ideologies: Communism, anarchism, nationalism. As political ideologies, they have manifestations which range from the mild and almost academic, or the acceptably programmatic, to the extremist and terrorist. Some Islamists are engaged in a moral critique – an argument about the right way of living and organising Muslim societies – while others run political parties in Muslim countries with a view to capturing political power.[8] As many of these countries, especially in the Middle East, are non-democratic and authoritarian, such political parties are clandestine and conspiratorial.

There are nationalist liberation movements where Muslims are the oppressed community, often in a majority, and they use Islamic symbols as mobilising devices. One such device is to give the group a name with holy connotations, such as Lashkar-e-Toiba (Army of the Faithful), a Pakistani group fighting for Kashmir to belong to Pakistan. They often resort to violent attacks, which are now being increasingly labelled as terrorist. These forms of Islamism overlap with, but have to be kept distinct from, the ideological groups whose programme is terrorism, and whose canvas is not national or territorial, but global. They have no territorial goal for winning power, unless their desire for a global Islamic society is taken seriously.

At the risk of oversimplifying, we can label the mildest form as *Moral Islamism*, where the idea is to urge a more pious or orthodox living style on Muslims. The next stage is *National* (or *Political*) *Islamism*, which is a political programme for capturing power within a Muslim country and changing its official policy to conform to religious tenets such as the Sharia. The form that most concerns us is *Global Islamism*.

Global Islamism has arrived at a time when other forces have been at work globalising the world. Internet and mobile telephony made possible by satellite technology, rapid deregulation and liberalising of international capital movements and progressive dismantling of tariff barriers, vast movements of legal and illegal immigrants and the growing evil of human trafficking, clandestine trade in drugs and money-laundering, the cheapening of lethal arms and the ease with which they are traded across borders – all have made the world of the last ten or fifteen years very different from the previous thirty years. Global Islamism and the terror it has fostered, along with drugs and arms and human trafficking, inhabit the dark side of globalisation.

It is necessary to understand the true nature of Global Islamism if we are to defeat it, since otherwise its lethal effects will spread and accelerate. It is also important not to get confused with problems of Islam as a *faith* or Muslims as a *people*. Whatever their habits of living, believing and worshipping, in whichever society they choose to inhabit, issues are raised which we all need to debate and discuss – concering dress, forced marriage, the notion of honour killing, or faith schools. Muslims, as all other communities, bring their own unique qualities to our lives in music, poetry, art and sculpture, dress and fashion, and habits of charity; just as they bring habits of life and thought which many may find strange, and sometimes disagreeable. These things are not my immediate concern as they do not connect with the ideology of the new terror.

We have to separate, therefore, the issue of integration or assimilation of Muslims, as of many other communities into modern societies, from the question of how to combat the ideology, which is lethal. Global Islamism has to be understood in the same way as Communism or Nazism when they became terrorist programmes. Inasmuch as no state power has sponsored Global Islamism (though the Taliban regime in Afghanistan came close), we also have to study the parallels with anarchism, since it has been an entirely stateless and decentralised violent action programme.

The war against terrorism has to be fought not just with intelligence and police and the armed forces but also at a cultural level. It may be useful here to make a distinction between fighting *terrorism* and fighting *terrorists*. The latter activity requires police, intelligence, secret surveillance, the army, and so on. Of course all of this has to be done within the rule of law and with due regard to human rights. This is because fighting the ideology of terrorism is not merely a police task. We have to understand the structure of the ideology and the story it tells us in defence of its actions. The story that Global Islamism tells involves the modern history of Europe over the last ten centuries, with America becoming a part of the story as an extension of Europe since its entry into the First World War. All ideologies have a story to relate. The story concerns a glorious past, a miserable present, an enemy who is responsible for the current lowly status of the people whom the ideologues claim to represent, and the programme of action which has to be undertaken if the miserable present is to be turned into a bright future which will restore the glorious past. Communism has such a story, as we shall see below, as does anarchism. Nationalism has a separate such story for each nation.

Some of the ideologies do not need to be fought to the death. Nationalism, despite its many ugly manifestations, has continued to have positive effects and is still a potent force in world politics. It has an unfinished agenda. Anarchism has been rendered harmless from what it was in the nineteenth and early twentieth centuries.[9] Communism has been defeated in its central manifestation as the USSR, though it still survives in China and North Korea, and is possibly on its last legs in Cuba. But the appeal of the non-terrorist version of Communism is still potent in Venezuela and India. Global Islamism is the enemy we have to concentrate on; not all Islamism and certainly not Islam. The war is not against Muslim fundamentalism any more than against Christian, Hindu or Jewish fundamentalism. This is not to deny that some people and parties will want to resist the appeal of all kinds of fundamentalism. But that would be the subject of a different sort of analysis.

The chapter immediately following this introduction sketches the history of events over the last three and a half decades that have made Global Islamism the spectre it has become. It is a well-cultivated field and I shall only give such details as are necessary to understand the nature of the problem we are fighting. The third chapter discusses the nature of ideologies in general and outlines the anatomy of an ideology. The emphasis is, of course, not on all ideologies, but on those that have been deployed for the political end of winning and retaining power. The fourth chapter deals with the history of Islam and of Muslim societies. Here again much is known and I only need to highlight that which is needed to illuminate Global Islamism. Then follows a chapter on the ideology of Global Islamism. The story it has to tell revisits some of the themes from the history of Muslim societies related in the previous chapter. Once the ideology of Global Islamism has been understood we need to know how the other ideologies were successfully contained and made incapable of inflicting gross misery while surviving as philosophies or belief systems. This will help us find means for combating Global Islamism.

TWO

The Route to 9/11

'He confounded causes with effects more than was
excusable; the most distinguished propagandists
with impulsive bomb throwers; assumed organisation
where in the nature of things it could not exist;
spoke of the social revolutionary party one moment
as of a perfectly disciplined army, where the word of
chiefs was supreme, and at another as if it had been
the loosest association of desperate brigands that ever
camped in a mountain gorge.'

(The anarchist Verloc, listening to the diplomat
Vladimir, in Joseph Conrad, *The Secret Agent*)

The Spectre that Haunts Europe (and America)

The events that are the subject of our concern – the bombing of
the World Trade Center in February 1993 and again on 9/11; the
attack on the USS *Cole*; the bombing of US Embassy in Kenya;
the bombs in Bali, Madrid, Delhi, Sharm-el-Sheikh, London and

Amman – have their proximate origins thirty-plus years ago in 1973. The deeper roots go back to the First World War and even yet further down to the Crusades themselves. But let us look at the proximate cause in the first instance.

The last serious conflict between Israel and Arab states took place in 1973. The Yom Kippur War began well for the Arabs but ended in defeat. There was also, however, a reassertion of Arab economic power as the Organisation of Petroleum Exporting Countries (OPEC) quadrupled the price of crude oil. Not all members of OPEC were Arab countries, but many were. Iran, a non-Arab Muslim country with Shi'a rather than Sunni followers, was also an important member; its ruler, the Shah, was an ambitious and pro-Western leader. The quadrupling of the oil price was a huge shock for the oil-dependent Western economies and it cost them 5 per cent of their national income, which was transferred to the OPEC countries, mainly Saudi Arabia, the Gulf Emirates and Iran. It was the largest such transfer in recent history. It amounted to $60 billion at 1972 prices, and at today's prices about ten times that amount.

The quadrupling of the oil price – the oil shock as it came to be known – was perhaps overdue. The price of a barrel of crude had not changed for nearly 50 years, while inflation had been accelerating in the USA and elsewhere since 1939. In the immediate aftermath, it triggered stagflation, a combination of high inflation and high unemployment, in many developed countries. In the longer run, though, it helped them adopt better energy-saving technologies. Yet it was meant as a punishment for Western support of Israel, whose triumphant, defiant presence was a sore point for the Arab countries. The Arab countries had tried three times to 'drive Israel into the sea'. In 1948, at the start of Israel's existence, they had been repulsed. In 1967, under the charismatic leadership of Gamal Abdel Nasser, they had tried again and lost. In 1973 they surprised the Israelis, but after some success again failed.

The 1973 defeat led to a deep soul-searching in the Middle East among Muslims. They did not abandon their hatred of Israel. They sought the reasons for the continuing humiliation they suffered. The problem was not Israel itself, but what it represented to the Muslims of the Middle East. Its presence was a constant reminder to Muslims of their sad history during the previous hundred years. All of the Arab Middle East had once belonged to the Ottoman Empire, the last of the great Muslim empires and the last one whose head also claimed to have supreme religious authority as the caliph or the *khalifa*.

A *khalifa* is a successor to the Prophet, the Messenger of God, Muhammad. The first four caliphs – Abu Bakr, Umar, Usman (Uthman) and Ali are taken to be a select group – *al-khulafa al-rashidun* (the rightly guided caliphs) as they were contemporaries as well as relatives of the Prophet.[10] On the death of the Prophet, as he had no male heir, the succession was an issue to be decided by the then small Muslim community, which consisted of his companions (*muhajirun*) and his supporters (*ansar*). The succession had to be from among the Quraysh, the tribe to which Muhammad belonged. At a large, somewhat loosely organised, meeting, a *saqifah*, where the companions and the followers had gathered upon hearing of the death of Muhammad, his father-in-law Abu Bakr claimed the first succession and he was chosen by the gathered crowd. Umar, who was also at the meeting, had an equally valid claim on grounds of nearness to the Prophet, but he was willing to concede to Abu

Bakr, who thus became the first caliph. The caliphate became the fount of authority for the Muslims since the first caliph was directly linked to the Prophet. As the first caliph, Abu Bakr chose to sit one rung below the *minbar*, the pulpit of authority where Muhammad sat. Abu Bakr, however, lived only one more year after his election as caliph. After Abu Bakr's death in 634 CE, Umar (r. 634–44) was the obvious choice. But subsequent succession proved problematical. Umar appointed a committee, a *shura*, of six people, which chose Usman (r. 644–56) after much hesitation. Usman's rule proved divisive and he was murdered. Ali, who was Muhammad's son-in-law and his first convert, had always thought that, being the Prophet's son-in-law and spiritually deeper than his rivals, he should have been the first caliph. Yet he had to wait until after Usman before he got his turn. A civil war immediately broke out between his predecessor Usman's party and himself. Ali (r. 656–61) was murdered, as was his son Hussayn. A schism was thus created around the caliphate of Ali; his supporters, the Shi'a, split from the Sunni caliphate, which became the mainstream.

Subsequent Sunni caliphs continued to trace their origin all the way back to the founder of Islam, the Prophet Muhammad himself. The person who removed Ali – Muawiyah – was the ruler of Baghdad. He founded the Umayyad dynasty with its capital in Damascus, since after him his line succeeded to the caliphate. The Abbasid caliphate, which traced its origin to Abbas, an uncle of Muhammad, succeeded the Umayyad in 749 and moved the capital to Baghdad. In 1517, the caliphate had passed from the Abbasid dynasty to the Ottoman, who traced their line back to Usman. The Ottoman Empire represented a continuity in (Sunni) Islam since its founding by Muhammad in the seventh century.

The defeat of the Ottoman Empire in the First World War had come at the end of a long series of reverses whereby other European powers, the Russian and Austro-Hungarian empires especially, had nibbled away at its territories. The glory days of the Empire were in the sixteenth and seventeenth centuries, with Suleiman the Magnificent a legend all over the world. But it had lost out to the West once the Industrial Revolution had come to Europe. Try as it might, the Ottoman Empire never recovered its position. In the European game of balance of power, it kept on losing out. Parts of the Empire – Egypt and Syria for instance – started breaking away, feigning allegiance but practically independent. The geography of the Middle East as it exists today had begun to take shape by the mid-nineteenth century.

The First World War had its main theatre on the borders of France and Germany and in the fields of Belgium, but it was also fought in the Eastern Mediterranean. At Gallipoli, Australian and New Zealand soldiers gave their lives, helping towards the final defeat of the Ottoman Empire. But well before the end of the war, the prospective dismemberment of the Empire was a subject of discussion among the Allied Powers, especially France and Great Britain, which were the major imperial powers and expected to be the victors, while the Austro-Hungarian and Ottoman empires were to be the losers. Somewhat in the manner of the pope who in the sixteenth century divided the New World (which he did not own) between Spain and Portugal, British and French governments started dividing up the Ottoman Empire into spheres of influence for themselves. But they did it secretly, telling their ally Russia but not anyone in Arabia. They had recruited a friend in Hussein, the sharif of Mecca, for fighting the Ottomans. Thus he became an ally and was promised by Sir Henry McMahon, the British high commissioner to Egypt, that after the war the Arabs would gain much autonomy. But unbeknown to him, Sir Mark Sykes of the British Foreign Office and Georges Picot of the Quai d'Orsay had drawn up an agreement, the now much-maligned Sykes–Picot Agreement of 16 May 1916, about how Britain and France would share out the remains of the Ottoman Empire in Arabia. After the October Revolution, the Bolsheviks published all the secret treaties and Sykes–Picot became public knowledge. Arabs felt betrayed, as did their friends like T.E. Lawrence, better known as Lawrence of Arabia. According to the Sykes–Picot Agreement, Iraq and Jordan were to go to Britain and Lebanon and Syria to France, Palestine was to be under an international regime, Jerusalem being the home of the holy places of three religions.

Even this arrangement for Palestine was reversed soon after the Sykes–Picot Agreement. Jerusalem fell to British forces and Lloyd George as the wartime prime minister was keen to retain British control. There was also a propaganda war being waged between the opposing camps for the European Jewish population. Balfour was keen to concede the demands which had been on the table for the Zionist movement to have a home in Palestine. Edwin Montagu, the only Jewish member of the Cabinet, was against this idea and Lord Curzon argued the Arab case. But at that time Arab national-ism looked a faraway, if not unlikely, prospect. So the Imperial War Cabinet declared on 31 October 1917 that

> The Secretary of State for Foreign Affairs to take a suitable op-portunity of making the following declaration of sympathy with the Zionist aspirations.

His Majesty's Government views with favour the establishment
in Palestine of a national home for the Jewish people, and will use its
best endeavours to facilitate the achievement of this object, it being
clearly understood that nothing shall be done which may prejudice
the civil and religious rights of existing non-Jewish communities in
Palestine, or the rights and political status enjoyed by Jews in any
other country.

Arthur Balfour the British foreign secretary, then embodied
this Cabinet resolution in a letter to Lord Rothschild. This is
how it became known as the Balfour Declaration. But for all the
controversy the Declaration has caused, it was just the last item
of twelve on the Cabinet's agenda that day. Grey, who had been
foreign secretary at the start of the war, had argued the case in
1916. Balfour's religiosity inclined him to be sympathetic to the
Zionist cause. In a remarkably prescient statement, he said in 1920
at a Zionist rally:

Palestine, great as the place it occupies in the history of the world,
is but a small and petty country looked at as a geographical unit...
But what are the requisites of such development in Palestine as may
accommodate an important section of the great race I am address-
ing? One is skill, knowledge, perseverance, enterprise; the other is
capital, and I am perfectly convinced that when you are talking of
the Jews you will find no want of any of these requisites.[11]

All that was left of the Ottoman Empire in 1918 was Anatolia,
and a small perch in Europe across the Bosphorous. All its Arab
territory was taken away at the Versailles Conference, and the
sultan was made to sign the Treaty of Sèvres in 1920. He did not
last long. There was a move to divest the sultan of his caliphate
and the caliphate was given to the sharif of Mecca, thus separating
for the first time the caliphate from the supreme Muslim ruler,

causing some consternation among the faithful everywhere. There was an agitation in India which was led by Mahatma Gandhi and the leaders of the Muslim community in India – Mohammad Ali and Shaukat Ali – to stop the British from interfering with this valuable heritage of Islam. The Khilafat agitation, as it was called proved to be futile. Hussein, the sharif of Mecca who had betrayed the sultan and become the new caliph, was defeated by the Saudi family who did not take up the caliphate themselves. The sultan was overthrown, and a republic was established in 1923. Kemal Atatürk was a moderniser, and he decreed a secular state for Turkey, as the remainder of the Ottoman Empire was to be called. Far from the British interfering with the caliphate, it was Atatürk who abolished it.

The victors may write history, and indeed have the luxury of forgetting it, but it is the losers who remember it. Muslims remember the Sykes–Picot Agreement when all in the Western chanceries have long forgotten it. The Balfour Declaration has always been a sore point for the Muslims of the Middle East. They choose perhaps not to know that the caliphate was abolished by a Turkish general who saw that religion was an obstacle to the modernisation of the Middle East.

The end of the Ottoman Empire is seen as the confirmation of the decline of the Muslims, the end of any hope of regaining the glories of the Muslim past. From the days in the seventh century when the religion was founded at the same time as the state by the Prophet, there had been an inseparable connection between the secular and the spiritual authority. Islam never witnessed the struggle over separation of church and state which Europe did. There was no notion of a secular authority to which Muslims could submit and be good Muslims. The challenge of being a good citizen or subject of a non-Islamic state and being a good Muslim has always been acute for Muslims. While the Ottoman Empire was there, Muslims living under non-Islamic regimes could console themselves that if they so wished they could go and live under the caliph. At worst, they could pray for him in their Friday prayers wherever they lived. After thirteen centuries, Muslims found themselves for the first time without a spiritual and secular authority which defined the global Muslim community – the *umma*. From now on Muslims would have to define the fountain of their loyalty. The end of the caliphate caused a crisis in the Sunni Muslim *umma*. 'Were it not for the caliph and the Qur'an he recites, people would have no judgements established for them and no communal worship.'[12] The end of the Ottoman Empire and the end of the caliphate are serious matters for the Sunni Muslim faithful.

This is so because Mecca is their spiritual home, and Mecca, indeed the great holy lands Hijaz, was in the Ottoman Empire. India was a part of Al-Hind, which stretched east of Mecca all the way to Indonesia. The fortunes of the Ottoman Empire concerned the Muslims of India and the rest of Al-Hind as well. A Muslim living under the British yoke in India looked to the Ottoman emperor as his caliph, mentioned him in his Friday prayers, and thought of the Empire as somewhere he could be under a Muslim ruler if he so wished. Indeed, during 1857, when the Indian Army units in Bengal and United Provinces rose up against the British, Muslim loyalty was sought by the British by appealing to the Ottoman emperor to instruct Muslims not to rebel. The emperor was happy to oblige as the British had been helpful to him in the Crimean War.

The sorry state of the Empire was known even before the First World War of course. Muhammad Iqbal was a major poet of Persian and Urdu, a modernist lawyer who practised in London and Lahore. He is the author of Pakistan's national anthem but also of a paean to India (Hindustan) which was popular enough to be sung at the fiftieth anniversary of Independence in the Indian houses of parliament. In 1909, he wrote a beautiful poem entitled *Shikwa* (*Complaint*), which is a complaint, almost a rebuke, by a faithful Muslim to Allah for the sorry state in which he has allowed his faithful to fall in recent times.[13] It has an evocative beginning:

> Why must I forever lose, forever forgo profit that is my due.
> Sunk in the gloom of evenings past, no plans for the morrow pursue,
> Why must I all attentive be to the nightingale's lament,
> Friend, am I as dumb as a flower? Must I remain silent?
> My theme makes me bold, makes my tongue more eloquent,
> Dust be in my mouth, against Allah I make complaint. (28)

After this opening gambit, Iqbal recalls how with God's inspiration Muslims had gone across the world spreading his word at the point of the sword and gaining glory for his name.

> Of all the brave warriors, there were none but only we,
> Who fought Your battles on land and often on the sea.
> Our calls to prayer rang out from the churches of European lands
> And floated across Africa's scorching desert sands.
> We ruled the world, but regal glories our eyes disdained,
> Under the shades of glittering sabres Your creed we proclaimed. (33)

Why then, he asks, had Allah now chosen to let them sink into the abyss that they found themselves in.

> Our complaint is not that they are rich, that their coffers overflow:
> They who have no manners and of polite speech nothing know.

What injustice! Here and now are houris and palaces to infidels
   given;
While the poor Muslim is promised houris only after he goes to
   heaven.
Neither favour nor kindness is shown towards us anymore;
Where is the affection You showed us in the days of yore? (43)

Shikwa is a bold experiment for a Muslim poet inasmuch as it
challenges Allah and holds him to account. We see in it Muslim
pride in past glories and triumphs as Islam spread across Europe
and Africa by the sword, and the contrast with the present degra-
dation of Muslims and the prosperity of the infidels.

A few years after his 1909 poem, in 1913, Iqbal penned God's
reply – *Jawab-e-Shikwa* (*Reply to the Complaint*). In the reply, he
had God say that he had not abandoned his faithful but had been
abandoned by them.

There were days when this very Allah you regarded as sublime;
The tulip of Islam was the pride of the desert in blossom time.
There were days when every Muslim loved the only Allah he knew;
Once upon a time He was your beloved; the same Beloved you now
   call untrue.
Now go and pledge your faith to serve some local deity
And confine Muhammad's following to some one locality. (68)

They had veered from the true path he had set for them in the
message he had given his messenger, the Prophet Muhammad.
They had fallen low even in worldly arts.

The only people in the world of every skill bereft are you.
The only race which cares not how it fouls its nest are you.
Haystacks that within them conceal the lightning's fire are you.
Who live by selling tombs of their sires are you.
If as traders of tombstones you have earned such renown,
What is there to stop you trading in gods made of stone? (70)

But God does not disappoint. The poem ends by Allah saying that
Muslims had the key for their renaissance in their own hands, and
it was to return to Him.

> With reason as your shield and the sword of love in your hand,
> Servant of God! The leadership of the world is at your command.
> The cry 'Allah-o-Akbar' destroys all except God; it is a fire.
> If you are true Muslims, your destiny is to grasp what you aspire.
> If you break not faith with Muhammad. We shall always be with you;
> What is this miserable world? To write the world's history, pen and
>   tablet we offer you. (96)

Iqbal's poems are relevant for various reasons. First, they
give a vivid impression of how much wider the (Sunni) Muslim
community – the *umma* – was which regarded itself as belonging
to the Empire, to the caliphate. The reason, as we saw above, was
the control of the holy land of Mecca and Medina which the Ottoman emperor had. The question of who rules over these lands,
over the Hijaz, is of concern to Muslims everywhere. The other
most holy place is of course Jerusalem. It was Jerusalem which was
thrown open to 'alien' rule just at the time the caliphate ended.
The British had a mandate in Palestine. The holy lands went under
the control of the Saud family.

   In theory, Islam does not recognise kingship as such because
all authority flows from the Prophet. This is a normative position
– things as they ought to be. In recent discussions of Islam, this
normative position has often been conflated with the actual one.
In fact, of course, even as the Muslim armies spread across Asia
and Europe, no single political power controlled all the faithful. A
quarrel over the succession to the Prophet had alienated the followers of Ali, whose martyrdom became the cause of the schism that
determined that the Shi'a would not be part of the same community

as the Sunnis. The caliph (of the Sunnis) sat in Baghdad for a few centuries and then in Istanbul until 1924. But the caliph's authority was a remote one and not as rigidly enforced as that of a tsar. Muslims have lived under different political authorities, Muslim and non-Muslim. In India, for instance, the Mughals, who ruled between the 1520s and the 1750s, did not formally acknowledge the supremacy of the Ottoman emperor but nor did they claim the universal caliphate. The caliph did not enforce obedience but expected it as part of his Qur'anic sanction.

There is also an unacknowledged fact that while Islam is a unitarian religion – one God, one Book, one Prophet – it has developed in different regions with local variations. Thus Islam in the Indian subcontinent has absorbed some Hindu influences more via Sufi teachings than directly. This has not prevented the growth of some fine theological scholarship in the Deobandi school, which grew as a response to the challenge of modernity in the late nineteenth century. But in the Philippines or Malaysia local religions have been absorbed into Muslim practices. It is with globalisation that there has arisen a drive, a Moral Islamist drive, to impose a uniformity on Muslim practices everywhere. Yet much of the agony of Muslim defeatism is confined to Arabia and is not universal.

Nowadays much is made of the *umma* as a global community of Muslims, which is in some sense autonomous. This is a reconstruction of history. The Muslim *umma* is the same sort of notion as Christendom. It may once have been real, especially for those inside the Ottoman Empire, but now it is a myth re-created for rhetorical purposes as and when it is needed for political convenience.

It may be helpful to think of the importance of the caliphate by analogy with the state of Christendom before Luther's rebellion.

The pope was the spiritual leader of the Church and as such claimed power over Christian kings. He dispensed favours, such as annulment of marriage (where Henry VIII fell foul), absolved sins, and sometimes excommunicated recalcitrant Christians, condemning them to purgatory. Imagine the Ottoman emperor winning the Battle of Lepanto in 1571 and then taking over Rome and abolishing the papacy. What would Christians have done in that case?

Reform and Revival in Arabia

It is this long history of the caliphate that was present in the Muslim imagination when once again the Arab armies were humiliated. There was the need for a renaissance, which in 1973 inaugurated the religious revival in Arabia. The challenge of modernity had posed itself to the Muslims as it had hit Christians in the West first of all and then other religious communities – the Hindus, for instance – elsewhere. Christians fought their battle of modernity at home: the battle to reconcile the text of the Bible with the assaults of Reason and Science. (As the current American debate on Darwin shows, the battle is not over yet for some Christians.) Other religions experienced the battle as part of a response to imperialism, which asserted its superiority not only in arms and technology but in education and religion as well. While the responses had local nuances, they all took the shape of revival and/or reform. There were some who wanted to go back to the ancient traditions, the received text, and purify the faithful. Others saw that they had to jettison a lot of the old baggage and reform the religion – 'Christianise' it, as it were. In India, for example, the battle merged with the anti-colonial struggle for the two religious communities.

There had been attempts at reform and modernisation across the Middle East. There were those who wanted to westernise the Muslim societies; Atatürk is a prime example of this tendency. He was not just a reformist but was strongly opposed to religion, especially Islam. His secularism was strongly anti-religious, and being modern meant being pro-Western. The Shah of Iran, who was dethroned in 1979 by the Islamic Revolution, was another such ruler whose drive for modernity involved waging a war against Islam. Thus the experience of modernity for Muslims in Turkey and Iran was to perceive westernisation as virulently anti-Islamic. This need not have been the case, but it was. The influence of socialism was also felt after the October Revolution in Russia. Secular socialist parties like the Ba'ath Party were one such force. Kingdoms were overthrown and republics declared in Iraq, Syria, Libya and Egypt in the decades after the Second World War. The secular socialist parties downplayed the religious question until after 1973. Modernisation was to be the path of the renaissance in Arabia.

The defeat of 1973 put paid to those dreams. Reform was devalued. The answer had to be revival, going back to the Holy Qur'an, to the ways of the Prophet and the original followers, the *Salafiya*. The community had to abide by the Sharia, the law of proper behaviour as set down from early times. The task was to reject the blandishments of modern Western culture, and repurify Muslims, if the glory of the *umma* was to be restored. By its nature, this was not a nationalist but a supranational demand. It did not and could not have a territorial focus as many of the nations in the Middle East were ruled by Muslim leaders anyway. These regimes had to be made more Islamic not just Muslim. But beyond that the entire group of Muslim nations of the region had to be united in some sort of a revival against a common enemy. The attempts that had been made previously by secular leaders such as Nasser to create a United Arab Republic had all failed. Arabia was not a secular political unity; it could, however, be made a spiritual unity.

If that was the need of the hour, help was at hand. The house of Saud had a kingdom in central Arabia since at least the seventeenth century. Early in its formation, the king had made a pact with a holy man, Muhammad ibn Abd al-Wahhab, and agreed to establish a kingdom based on Sharia. The movement that al-Wahhab represented was heir to a long tradition going back five centuries of previous examination of the state of the *umma*. There had been corruption and backsliding even as the political and military power of Muslim emperors was unquestioned. The lesson was to go back to the simple religion of the Prophet and his early associates. As Ibn Taymiyya, a fourteenth-century philosopher, is said to have described it, 'The true Muslim was he who had faith: not simply acceptance of the revealed God, but action in accordance with God's revealed will.'[14] The way to learn about God's revealed will was to consult a hierarchy of authorities:

> Ibn Taymiyya first of all looked to the Qur'an, understood strictly and literally, then to the Hadith (the tradition of what the Prophet had said or done), then to the Companions of the Prophet whose consensus had a validity equal to the Hadith. (180)

Wahabbism was a literal textual approach to religion, based on such a hierarchy of authorities. It committed the Saudi kings to create a kingdom strictly following the purest interpretation of the authoritative texts. The text of the Qur'an in Islam has a different status from that of the Bible in Christianity. The Qur'an is considered to be the revealed word of God, without any intermediation.

It is said to have been heard by Muhammad. As Muhammad was chosen by Allah to be his messenger, his sayings and doings had a high status, next only to the Qur'an itself. After that came the Companions, the original group who had received the word from Muhammad and travelled with him as he was persecuted for his beliefs and stayed with him till his hour of triumph. The Bible, by contrast, is more like news gathered by a pool of reporters over a long period of time. The first five books of the Old Testament are said to have been written by Moses. But there is much more in the Old Testament that is a mixture of the practical (food taboos), history of the Jewish people and spiritual teachings. The Bible acquires some immediacy in the Gospels, but even they were written down a generation after the Crucifixion. Also the text of the Qur'an has not been subjected to the sort of scholastic exegesis as the Bible has been. Even such attempts that have been made very recently by Western scholars have not been welcome among the faithful.[15]

Since it is a frequent practice to look askance at Muslim traditions, or alternatively to fall overboard about their uniqueness, it may be said that the Puritans who left the shores of England and sailed to Massachussets in the seventeenth century and established their colony were not unlike the Wahabbis. Textual literalness defines a fundamentalist, as much among Christians as among the Muslims. There are political parties even today in Israel's Knesset which hold to a literal interpretation of the holy texts of Judaism. Many fundamentalist Christians in the USA agree with them about the Biblical entitlement the Jews have to territories across Israel and Palestine.

The importance of the eighteenth-century alliance with Wahabbism made by the Saudi royal family was to have its consequences in the late twentieth century. The Saudi royal family now controlled the holy cities of Mecca and Medina. This gave a special status in Islam. Since the need was for a re-purification of the Muslims and since the Saudi royal family had the windfall of an enormous quantity of petrodollars, it had both the will and the means to spread the word of God among the Muslims. They made an internationally widespread commitment to open madrasas which would teach young Muslims to read the Qur'an, rather like Sunday schools where Christian children are sent to read the Bible. These madrasas are free.

In many countries with a large Muslim population, most of which are among the poorer Third World countries, these madrasas were often the only schools children could attend. In Pakistan, for example, there are reported to be more than 6,000 of them educating 800,000 students.[16] Since the Qur'an is in Arabic, they all learn to recite, if not read, the Qur'an. But along with the reading and recitation, the teachers in charge also impart their philosophy to their charges. After all, that is what all teachers do. Who takes charge of such schools depends very much on local variations among Muslim religious teachers, the imams.

Thus it was that in Pakistan the dominant influence came from a school of Islamic theology known as the Deobandi school.[17] The challenge of modernity, discussed above, had impacted on Indian Muslims in the nineteenth century as much as on Hindus and on Muslims elsewhere. There was a reformist call for Indian Muslims to embrace Western education by Sir Syed Ahmad, who established the Anglo-Oriental College. Later it became the Aligarh Muslim University, which is still flourishing. But the revivalist response was pioneered by a group of scholars from the village of Deoband.

They started with a desire to teach learning from the West while also going back to a strict, literal interpretation of the Qur'an. They had twelve madrasas with paid teachers and a proper curriculum in 1879. By the time the Saudis were getting active, there were already 7,000 such schools across India and Pakistan (Burke 2003: 93). Their students were called *taliban*.

We have to put the madrasa issue in some perspective. They are not 'terror schools', as they have been called in some British newspapers after the 7/7 bombings in London. They are simple, well-meaning schools that help to teach religion to the children. They are part of a tradition going back centuries; after all, it is Islam's respect for learning that preserved and transmitted classical Greek knowledge via the Byzantine civilisation to Renaissance Europe. The teaching tradition in such schools varies by region and culture. There are many local variations, even though Islam is a single book/single God religion. Thus in South Asia the religion developed in a much more syncretic fashion, interacting with Hinduism, than in the Middle East. In Andalucia, where Muslims were dominant for half a millennium, there was much interaction between Jews, Christians and Muslims.

There were schools of Islamic teaching which did not agree with the Deobandi. A scholar such as Maulana Abul Kalam Azad managed to combine being a leading theologian and a secular nationalist in the Congress Party in India. He became India's education minister for the first thirteen years after Independence and played a vital role in the expansion of modern education at all levels.

The Saudi effort has, however, advanced a revivalist orthodox position and set back the modernising tendencies in Islam. It fed the dissatisfaction with the secular socialist efforts to modernise the Middle East. There arose a movement in many Muslim countries that made efforts to replace ruling governments by those adhering to a purer Islamic path. This happened early on in Egypt while it was formally a part of the Ottoman Empire but under British tutelage. The Muslim Brotherhood was a movement that wanted to challenge the then ruler and compel him to make Egypt a society based on Sharia, rather like Saudi Arabia.

Pakistan: A Muslim not an Islamic Nation

A more recent example is Pakistan, which was perhaps the first modern independent Muslim state. It was set up by the partitioning of British India into India and Pakistan and integrating such native states as within each territory. (Kashmir, a native kingdom with a Hindu king and a Muslim majority population, which bordered both India and Pakistan, refused to join either until it was much too late. An incursion of irregulars from Pakistan threatened the king, whereupon he joined India. A war between India and Pakistan ended with a plea to the UN for mediation. Kashmir has proved to be a bone of contention between the two ever since.) The principle of the partition was that majority Muslim provinces of British India went to Pakistan, and the rest to India. This split the Muslim population of pre-Independence India roughly into two equal parts. This was because the majority of Muslims lived in populous provinces where they were in a minority, and the majority Muslim provinces were sparsely populated. Two populous provinces, Punjab and Bengal, were split between the two countries.

Mohammad Ali Jinnah, the founder of Pakistan, was a secular westernised nationalist of the type who flourished in the Indian

Congress Party before Gandhi took it over. He drank alcohol, ate pork and married a Parsee woman. His transformation from a modern Anglophile to the founder of a Muslim nation-state is in itself a fascinating story. He started with a desire to unite Hindus and Muslims despite attempts on the part of many British and some Muslim politicians to divide them. Once Gandhi gave a religious, albeit ecumenical, colour to the ideology of the Indian independence movement, Jinnah withdrew from the Congress Party and retired to London to practise law. Congress in his view had become a Hindu organisation. Faced with the prospect of a majoritarian democratic state in post-British India, he began to argue that there were two nations – one Hindu and one Muslim. At one level, this could have been a demand for protection of minority status and rights. But in the 1940s this was not understood as we now understand the importance of giving minorities a veto over their rights. In Northern Ireland, for example, there was a permanent majority of Protestants facing a permanent minority of Catholics. The latter would be the majority and the former a minority if the two parts of Ireland were to be united. Both the communities were anxious about the preservation of their rights. So the Belfast Agreement of Easter 1998 gave each community a veto protecting their rights. But in the mid-1940s when negotiations for India's independence were being held, few understood that this was possible. So the two nations became two nation-states, with the Muslim 'nation' split between the two.[18]

Jinnah got his nation-state and even called it the Islamic Republic of Pakistan, but he had no intention of making it an Islamic state in the sense of the Wahabbis or the Deobandis. But there were others who did want to make Pakistan a model Muslim state.

Maulana Maududi was one such articulate person, who 'turned religion into an ideology of political struggle'.[19] His political party Jamaat-i-Islami has a platform of turning Pakistan into a purer Muslim state.

Zia ul-Haq was the army Chief of Staff of Pakistan in the 1970s; like some of his predecessors, he removed the elected leader – Zulfikar Ali Bhutto – and installed himself as president. He did more to propel Pakistan towards an Islamic state than any previous Pakistani leader, though more out of cynicism than piety. He needed the orthodox forces to contain the secular democratic elements in Pakistan if he was to survive. The reputation of the Pakistan Army was at a low ebb, since in 1971 it had lost the battle in East Pakistan to India and the Bangladeshi guerrilla army, the Mukti Bahini. But Zia was lucky: another war in his neighbourhood rescued him.

The Afghan Adventure

One common approach to this complex issue is to see our current problems as unfinished business of the First World War. The break-up of the Austro-Hungarian Empire created the countries in the Balkans, which united as Yugoslavia for four decades after 1945 but disintegrated soon after the death of Tito, the country's charismatic leader. The problem of the break-up of Yugoslavia occupied the world through much of the 1990s. The dissolution of the Ottoman Empire is central to our story in the way it created a fragmented Arabia and the opportunity for a homeland for the Jews. The collapse of the Romanov empire was arrested and reversed thanks to Lenin and his Bolshevik Revolution. The USSR collaborated with the Anglo-US alliance in the Second World War. But the Cold War started soon after 1945 and the last remaining empire in Europe was now engaged in a war on economic, cultural and nuclear fronts with the West.

The USSR was losing the economic war, though this did not become clear until the late 1960s. In the 1970s the capitalist West was caught in stagflation but the Communist East had its own problems of lack of innovation and faltering productivity growth. The West got out of its problems by severe restructuring and jettisoning the Keynesian paradigm. But the USSR could not re-structure. Nor could it reduce its international commitments, as Britain had to learn to do after the Suez adventure. In the midst of its troubles, it decided to heed the call of the Communist Party of Afghanistan, which had overthrown the King. The entry of the Soviet Army into Afghanistan made that region the hottest spot in the Cold War in the 1980s.[20]

The USA decided to use Pakistan as the entry point for guer-rillas who would undermine the Soviet-backed Afghan regime. Unlike the Vietnam War, the campaign against the Soviet army in Afghanistan was to be carried out not by American soldiers but by the volunteer fighters – mujahideen. The CIA could use the ISI of Pakistan as an agency, secretive like itself, but with Zia's full backing to route arms and money to these volunteers. They came from across the *umma* – young Muslim boys and men – and they formed an army which, along with some Afghan warlords such as Gulbuddin Hekmatyar, was to overthrow the regime.

In 1979, an Islamic Revolution overturned the order in Iran. The Shah had attempted to modernise Iranian society as Atatürk had tried with Turkey. But his White Revolution came a cropper, and he was thrown out by one of the most significant Islamic personalities of the twentieth century: Ayatollah Ruholla Khomeini. Khomeini had been conducting a campaign against the Shah since the early 1960s from Najaf in Iraq, and later from Paris. He was able to mobilise the lower-middle-class urban population who resented the westernised secular and rich elite surrounding the Shah. Khomeini's Revolution was Islamic, albeit a Shi'a one. It was total. Just as the October Revolution led to Russia's withdrawal for a while from international circles, Khomeini was determined to take Iran completely out of any Western camp and rebuild it along pure Islamic lines. Iran remains today a theocracy which overrides the civilian democratic apparatus.

The Iranian Revolution was bogged down in a long war with its neighbour Iraq, which was armed and encouraged by Western powers to bring Khomeini down. It was a gruelling eight-year war, which was largely ignored by the Western media – as they do with all wars so long as no Western army is involved in active fighting. The media ignored the war in Afghanistan for the same reason. The humanitarian concerns of Western media and intellectuals are very parochial: there is indignation only where Western soldiers are involved in killing or being killed in any part of the world. If 'natives' are killing each other somewhere remote, there is total neglect.

It was in the Afghan adventure that Osama Bin Laden cut his teeth. It was perhaps Khomeini's example which gave him the rhetorical idea of how to challenge the West. The collapse of the Soviet intervention in Afghanistan happened even faster than that of US intervention in Vietnam. Osama Bin Laden could see that the Great Powers could be defeated by determined guerrilla armies.

He left Afghanistan soon after the collapse but was to come back when the Taliban had displaced the warlords who had been in the advance guard of the battle against the Soviet forces.

The Iranian Revolution, the collapse of the Soviet empire and the detritus of the Ottoman Empire converged when Iraq invaded Kuwait in 1990. The Iran–Iraq war had ended in an inconclusive way with both sides exhausted. The Americans used Saddam in an attempt to bring down their Iranian enemy, but failed. In the meantime their arch enemy Soviet Union had fallen apart, partly thanks to the Muslim mujahideen. The Iraqi invasion of Kuwait provided a blueprint for the New World Order which George Bush Sr. had welcomed. America was now the only superpower, and it would draw the contours of the new order according to its liking.

It was not so much the Iraqi invasion of Kuwait but its premonition as to what Saddam could do to the many smaller states of the Gulf area that provided the rationale by which American troops were allowed to be stationed on Saudi Arabian soil in 1990 – the decisive event of the new era of Islamist terrorism. The presence of non-Muslim troops on Hijaz land was the spark that inspired Bin Laden to launch his long war against the Americans. From the abolition of the caliphate to the occupation of the holy lands by non-Muslim troops was a steep decline. This was the abyss. For the Islamist ideologue that Osama Bin Laden had now become, this was more than he could tolerate. The Saudi royal family, in his view, had besmirched itself and the holy land. It had to be removed. A series of attempts to attack the American mainland and American interests abroad began.

This is the background against which the New Terrorism has to be understood. Across the Muslim world in Arabia as in Europe,

Asia, Africa and North America, there has been a move for Muslims to adhere more closely to a pious lifestyle, for women to adopt modest dress, for prayers in the newly built mosques and to live a life by the book, the Holy Qur'an. There was already pressure on Muslim countries to adopt Sharia and follow the path of the righteous even before 1991. This was a political Islamist movement in individual Muslim countries but conducted separately in each. Egypt, Algeria, Pakistan, Indonesia, Malaysia have all been sub-ject to such a political movement. What Bin Laden fashioned was a Global Islamist movement where the enemy was no longer the particular national government. The enemy was the West, which had intruded on Jerusalem in 1918, and now, in 1991, in the Hijaz itself. The caliphate was gone long ago as part of the same process. This was, Bin Laden claimed, not the crisis of a single Muslim country but of the *umma* itself.

What enabled Bin Laden to leverage a number of local battles be-tween the religious parties and the secular authorities into a global struggle was the quite independent developments that we now call globalisation. This was another strand of the forces unleashed by 1973 and the oil shock. It led to a loss of competitiveness for West-ern manufacturing enterprises and the movement of manufacturing away from the Western economies. It also led to a proliferation of financial innovations and institutions as the world tried to absorb the $60 billion of petrodollars which sat in Western banks and had to be loaned out to Third World governments. Western govern-ments soon retrenched, abandoned Keynesian policies and squeezed inflation out of their economies. In the process the two Anglo-Saxon economies, the USA and the UK, began to deregulate capital movements so that it started to flow freely to all parts of the world where there were market economies. Technological developments in information processing, telecommunications and transport at the same time had made travel and communications cheap beyond imagination. The World Wide Web arrived in the 1990s and gave even the most isolated individual access to information about the means of terror and enabled contact with friends in any part of the world.

The oil shock also accelerated international migration, which had slowed down after the First World War and resumed after 1945 but was still limited. Full employment in the West had created a need for unskilled labour which the periphery of the British, Dutch and French empires was quite willing to provide. A diaspora was slowly growing in the West of people from the Third World. After 1973, the oil-exporting countries imported labour from South and Southeast Asia and North Africa. The deregulation of capital markets and the increasing liberalisation of trade for the rich countries also created a need for skilled immigrant labour. By the 1990s there were large diasporas in all the major metropolises of the developed countries. Many of them were Muslim.

The decline of the Soviet empire added to this transhumance. Yugoslavia had originally been part of the Ottoman Empire but had passed on to the Austro-Hungarian Empire. After 1918, the Balkans divided into many individual countries – Serbia, Croatia, Bosnia-Herzegovina, Slovenia. The unity which Tito won after 1945 for these states broke down after his death. In the 1990s, suddenly many in Western Europe became aware that there were European Muslims living in the Balkans and they were being systematically cleansed by their neighbours. In the break-up of the USSR, at the same time, many Muslim republics became autonomous in Central

Asia and by the Caspian Sea. But there were conflicts between and within these republics. Azerbaijan and Armenia, Georgia and Osetia are examples. Chechnya, which was an autonomous part of the Russian Republic, began a struggle for independence. Chechnya was Muslim. Suddenly there were national and international conflicts, with Muslim victims as well as Muslim fighters, in and around Europe.

The world thus became much more connected, and at the same time Muslims were made aware that they were victims of battles left over from centuries of European wars and from decolonisation. The Muslim diaspora in the West could communicate and empathise with their brethren's struggle across Europe and the Middle East. The Palestine problem had always been there. The Kashmir dispute had never been settled between India and Pakistan. To that were now added Chechnya, Bosnia-Herzegovina, Kosovo. There were other conflicts too, such as in Sudan between Christians and Muslims; in the Philippines, again between the same two communities; in Cyprus, which had been divided now for thirty years.

The recruitment of Muslim youth to fight in Afghanistan was the trigger for a floating army of young mujahideen who were willing to go after Afghanistan, to Chechnya, to Bosnia or to Kashmir. Here was an army not so much of mercenaries, like the French Foreign Legion, but of ideologically motivated youth. Travel was cheap and so was communication. Money could be wired anywhere. Arms were cheap as the Soviet Union began to unravel and the newly independent republics of the former Soviet Union were willing to export them.

The 1990s thus became not a peaceful decade thanks to the end of the Cold War but a series of forest fires across the world. It was as if the world had been waiting for the big European Struggle, which had been going on since 1914 through two world wars and the forty years of Cold War, to be settled so that the remaining unresolved issues of the twentieth century could surface. But while these separate fires continued to burn, a global story was put together by Osama Bin Laden which forms the ideology of Global Islamism. It is this ideology that we need to understand if we are to counter the new terror.

THREE

Religion and Ideology

'All idealisation makes life poorer. To beautify it is to take away its character of complexity – it is to destroy it. Leave that to the moralists, my boy. History is made by men, but they do not make it in their heads. The ideas that are born in their consciousness play an insignificant part in the march of events. History is dominated by the tool and the production – by the force of economic conditions. Capitalism has made socialism, and the laws made by the capitalism for the protection of property are responsible for anarchism. No one can tell what form the social organisation may take in the future. Then why indulge in prophetic phantasies?'

(Michaelis, the ticket-of-leave apostle in
Joseph Conrad, *The Secret Agent*)

The Nature of Ideology

Ideology is a word used quite loosely these days, often pejoratively. Often a contrast is made between ideology and pragmatism implying that ideology is somehow impractical and likely to be rigid in the face of practical problems. Ideology has also been associated through much of the twentieth century with the left. The American sociologist Daniel Bell published in 1960 what would become a very influential book, *The End of Ideology*, announcing the arrival of a new age in which politics was to be based not on ideologies or theories but on practical objectives. Alas, like many other predictions of social scientists, this one also proved to be premature. The 1960s saw the Civil Rights Movement in America, as well as the Student Movement in America and Europe which led to a revival of unorthodox brands of Marxism such as Trotskyism and Maoism. Later still in the 1970s and onwards, conservative philosophers surprised the world by coming out with articulate theories of how the world worked, how it ought to work and what had to be done to bridge the gap between the 'is' and the 'ought'.

Destutt de Tracy, during the French Revolution, invented the term *ideologie* to describe a new science of ideas, and its champions called 'ideologists'. He thought the science could be built on the basis of a theory of sensations and would be 'a part of zoology'. He had a theory of society and a programme of how to put it right. But after initial enthusiasm for his theories from the powers that be, he lost influence. Napoleon set the fashion for subsequent dictators in denouncing de Tracy and the 'ideologues'.[21]

Yet what de Tracy was describing was the new rational, Enlightenment approach to analysing the problems people face. He demonstrated the powers of abstraction or of theorising prior to tackling practical problems. Thus he had a theory of how the world worked and how human experience could be understood as a systematic outcome of prior causes rather than a result of random or divinely driven forces. His programme was designed to improve the human condition. He said that realising the programme would involve a 'struggle'. The programme would recruit followers and partisans committed to achieving it. There was to be an appeal to the general public, but the key actors were to be chosen with care. Here in essence is the template for many subsequent ideological programmes.

Religion and Ideology

A distinction is usually made between religion and ideology, though it is not a hard and fast one. It is still necessary both to make the distinction and to be aware that the fine line we draw may slip now and then as the situation evolves; what was once ideology could easily calcify into a religion (as Marxism did) or a religion could be put to ideological uses (as is the case with Global Islamism). Religion and ideology share many aspects, and, as each mutates, it takes on the characteristics of the other. One can say that they are both attempts to make sense of the world around us and to offer a programme for human action. Religion relies for its explanation on God or some such supernatural, irrational principle. Ideology, being a creature of the Enlightenment, relies on reason and a systematic study of causes to provide its explanation. To the extent that an ideology appeals to authority rather than reason, it partakes of religion. To the extent that a religion tries to reconcile its dogma with science, it takes on the form of an ideology. But both have been put to misuse in the sense of phases of violent rule.

Terror is now associated with secular ideologies. I shall attempt to show why Global Islamism should be treated as an ideology rather than a religion.

Religions are seen nowadays as by and large peaceable and spreading the message of love and harmony. But this has not always been the case. Religion can use the instrument of terror to enforce compliance when it is in power and fears dissidence. The Holy Inquisition is a prime example. Out of power, ideology can be meek and mild and be indistinguishable from academic philosophy. In the hands of the state, ideology can be lethal.

A programmatic reform of the human condition is not the invention of the French Revolution. Siddhartha who became Gautama the Buddha (the Enlightened One) preached a message in which the emphasis was on the good life here and now rather than on the supernatural or the other world. He also established a series of monasteries (*mathas*) and his message was carried on by the collective, the Sangha. There was a strong whiff of social reform and opposition to the then dominant Vedic ritualistic version of the Hindu religion. Siddhartha's was perhaps the first religion that was largely a social reform movement. It had an egalitarian inclusive philosophy and did not posit a supernatural god as the principal element. Given its non-deist outlook, Buddhism has often been considered as other than a religion. Of course after the Buddha's death, as his message spread across the world but especially to North and Southeast Asia, he himself was treated like a deity.

One could say that Jesus Christ and his followers were dedicated to reforming the Jewish society of their day, and that the Sermon on the Mount is a brief but powerful programmatic statement. The religious authority of the day – the Sanhedrin – certainly saw the programme as a threat and had Jesus punished by the civil power – the Romans. Jesus and his followers were just one of several such groups challenging the religious order and proclaiming a new millennium at that time.

Muhammad saw all around him corruption of religious practices, *jahiliya* as he called it. He found inspiration in what he heard from above, words recorded in the Qur'an. He went on to implement the most revolutionary cleansing of his contemporary society and set standards for subsequent behaviour. His followers spread across Arabia and then North Africa (Maghreb), followed by Mediterrannean Europe until they got to Spain. To the East, they reached India (Al-Hind). As they conquered their territories, they also converted many of the conquered people. Believing that theirs was the only true religion made the use of violence unproblematical for the new conquerors. What they did, they believed, was ordained by God.

The conversion of the many pagan and gentile peoples to Christianity was, in contrast to Islamic conversion, by and large, a peaceful effort. The Apostles, Saint Paul and his followers went around converting many Jews and others around the Mediterranean Europe. It was not until Emperor Constantine converted that Christianity became a state religion. Thus the image of Christians is a meek one. Islam was born as a state religion and powered by the sword as much as by the word in its quest for new followers. This association of Islam with militancy is useful to the modern-day terrorist.

Christianity itself turned into a doctrine for state terrorism only with the Inquisition. This was a reaction to the reconquest of Muslim Spain by the Christians in the fifteenth century. The Inquisition was a hunt for dissidents, for those who fell short of the ideological zeal of the Catholic Church. Dissidence was punished severely and violently. Religion and intolerance became synonymous.

The next significant phase began with the crisis in the Catholic Church in the sixteenth century. Girolamo Savonarola is credited with a programmatic credo to cleanse the Christian world of the impieties of his day in Italy. He anticipated much of Luther's later criticism about corruption in the Catholic Church. Savonarola preached in Florence a harsh and ascetic style of living, denouncing luxuries and loose living. He saw an Apocalypse coming as retribution for the sins of Italians in general and Florentines in particular. He clashed with the Medici, who ruled Florence, and with Pope Alexander VI. He won power over Florence briefly and implemented his puritanical programme with the help of the monks of his order. Finally the people turned against him and he was condemned to death.

Savonarola was thus the first 'ideological Christian'. He wanted to capture the state and use the power to make people lead a better, more virtuous life in accordance with Christian precepts. 'The enterprise was given a militant spirit; it was presented by Savonarola as being at one and the same time an outward struggle against papal corruption, the commercial ethos, and Renaissance Humanism, and an inward struggle against worldly ambitions and carnal desires' (*Encyclopaedia Britannica*). He was duly punished for that ambition but his harsh creed survived in Calvin and in the Puritans who came after him. The Calvinists ruled Geneva much as Savonarola had Florence but much more successfully and for much longer. Calvin formulated a doctrine, almost an ideology, from Christianity which had as its aim a total restructuring of society and of individual lives. His was a totalising doctrine; it left nothing out of account. But even so, unlike modern ideologies, its basis was in the Bible and the ultimate authority was divine rather than human.

The Puritans, who were prominent during the English Civil War, descended from the Calvinist tendency. They held strong views not only about the true doctrine of Christianity but also on how daily as well political life was to be conducted. These fierce democrats exiled themselves to New England to sow the seeds of American democracy. In their case religion came very close to a political ideology and a framework for organising society. Their support for education, especially for schools and colleges, helped the spread of the Enlightenment and eventually undermined the influence of religion, but that was an unintended consequence. However, the Puritans also exhibited intolerance, as when they hunted for witches among their own people, to say nothing of their rejection of rival Christian sects.

Ideology and Philosophy

The major change in the importance of secular ideology came not with the Reformation, which was still based on the Bible, but with the Enlightenment in the eighteenth century. Now a doctrine of society sought the reasons for its malaise in causes which can be shown to have systematically preceded the effect. David Hume was an early sceptic about the possibility of demonstrating causality, but he agreed with the rational methodology of the Enlightenment. God was displaced as the central principle of all causation. Nevertheless early ideologists shared with religion one characteristic in their theories. They seek a total explanation of the world's past, present and future, but one based in history, political economy and sociology. Two centuries later, Karl Popper, a leading philosopher of the twentieth century, was to castigate such totalising explanation as historicism.

Adam Smith was impressed by Newton's success in explaining the workings of the universe from a small number of first principles – gravity for one. He attempted a theory of history based on a notion of stages of development – a sequence of modes of subsistence. The stages began with hunting and gathering, followed by pastoralism, agriculture and then finally commerce. A central principle was that people had a propensity to 'truck and barter', and as they pursued their own interests social changes came about through the autonomous action of myriad individuals. Laws of property evolved over time, and systems of governance emerged. The best system of governance was one which gave protection to property in a rule-based framework and allowed maximum freedom to people to pursue their self-interest. Adam Smith called this the system of natural liberty, and argued that it was the best principle and that all nations should seek to establish it.

Smith was a philosopher rather than an ideologue, but even without his preaching he had enormous influence soon after the publication of his *An Inquiry into the Nature and Causes of the Wealth of Nations*. His doctrine of natural liberty (often wrongly labelled laissez-faire) is programmatic only in recommending the removal of obstacles to free commerce. He was a mild mannered man and had no desire to capture power. His philosophy was this-worldly and of the present rather than futuristic or millenarian. Even so, he had a hard time distancing himself from religion. While his friend David Hume openly declared his scepticism, Smith was at best a deist, denying revelation but not religion. His was an attempt to build a rational set of beliefs in religion. Ideology had yet a long time to go before it completely freed itself from religion.

Yet the idea of providing a theory of history and a trajectory for the future based on a study of the past caught on among philosophers. Hegel was the major philosopher of the early nineteenth century and his theory emphasised the growth of rational consciousness over time so that societies became self-consciously more and more aware of what was happening to them. This was the realisation of the Idea as it unfolded itself in a movement of self-awareness through time. Hegel's was a totalising (though not totalitarian) philosophy. It had its ramifications in politics, law, ethics. It was also forward-looking as well as an explanation of the past. The direction was upwards, the theme was one of progress. The future was better than the present.

It was thought by his young followers – Young Hegelians, as they called themselves – that Hegel was just rewriting the Christian story of the Second Coming but describing it as self-realisation of the Idea. Thus the glorious future was just a return to the golden past, which is often a strategy in constructing an ideology. Hegel was himself a good Protestant and all his life fairly conservative in his behaviour. The Prussian monarchy of the day did not take kindly to atheism or even Catholicism. For Hegel, Christianity was an evolved and superior religion and hence in step with the march of the Idea. So the Young Hegelians embarked on a critique of his philosophy, starting with religion. Ludwig Feuerbach (who was not strictly a Young Hegelian but a philosopher in his own right) was the first to insinuate the notion that God was a human creation. Around this time in the mid-1830s, the first biography of Jesus was written by David Friedrich Strauss (translated into English by novelist George Eliot), treating him as a human being rather than divine one, scandalising the pious. Biblical scholarship began to undermine simple faith. Religion was to be held to account by philosophy in an attempt to see if the world could not be explained without any recourse to the supernatural. Such was the programme of the Young Hegelians.

The most successful of all these attempts was by Karl Marx and Friedrich Engels, who in 1846 wrote their celebrated manuscript *The German Ideology*, which Marx said later they had 'abandoned to the gnawing criticism of the mice'. Marx was 28 years old at this time and Engles two years younger. This was an in-house battle among the Young Hegelians. Marx and Engels by now were thinking their way to new directions and were cutting off their ties to Hegel. The book was a critique of the Young Hegelians, who were developing the ideas of Hegel. While they were criticising religion, Marx and Engels completely rejected religion and build their theory of society on entirely secular grounds. This was the materialist theory of history or the theory of historical materialism. It was the first and most elaborate attempt at providing a theory of history and of society without in any way invoking God or any other supernatural or extra-rational agency.

The ideas in the abandoned manuscript surfaced in various abridged forms, most famously in the Preface to *A Contribution to the Critique of Political Economy*, which Marx wrote in 1859. The Preface contains a terse summary of the materialist theory of history, the foundation upon which Marx's theory of the dynamics of history was built. It offers a theory of the stages of history similar to but more complex than the one Adam Smith had proposed. But

by the time the Preface was published in 1859, Marx had already
become better known. This was because of another much shorter
book – indeed a pamphlet – that he and Engels had written. It was
not just a theory of history; it made history.

Marx and Engels followed up their abandoned tome on ideology
by publishing a short sharp essay for the Communist League in
1848 – *The Communist Manifesto*. It was this more than any other
work of theirs that launched Communism as an ideology. They
gave Communism a shape and a theory. They gave it a programme
and a dream.

The basic story was a distillation of Adam Smith's theory of
history as reworked through Hegel's philosophy and the post-
Hegelian critique in *The German Ideology*. Societies go through
stages, which were now called modes of production. There was
progress, but it involved a struggle between the producing classes
and the owning classes. There was primitive Communism at the
beginning, where no classes and no conflict existed. But after that
a succession of modes of production – ancient/slave, feudalism/
serfdom, and capitalism came. Each mode was succeeded by another
because it proved inadequate to capture the progress of ideas and
of technology. Capitalism, or the bourgeois mode, was the current
one and in it the conflict between the proletariat (the workers)
and the capitalists (the owners of the means of production) was
the central dynamic force. But capitalism, too, was destined to
pass. It would be followed by socialism and then Communism.
Under capitalism, the proletariat – the propertyless workers – were
exploited by the capitalists who owned the means of production
which the workers were employed to use to produce surplus value.
Socialism would come with the collapse of capitalism as a result of

its own internal contradictions. Class antagonism would end with the arrival of Communism; the prehistory of the world comes to an end. Henceforth people are in control of their own destinies.

Having written *The Communist Manifesto* in 1848, Marx and Engels found themselves at the losing end of a European revolution which tried to overthrow monarchies and establish republics. Back in the library of the British Museum, Marx worked out an elaborate economic theory of how capitalism was sustained by the exploitation of workers by capitalists. In the three volumes of his master work, *Capital*, he traced a sequence of crises and cycles as part of the dynamics of capitalism and foresaw a decline in profitability and an eventual breakdown of the capitalist system.[22]

Marx gave perhaps the best definition of ideology when he remarked in his *Theses on Feuerbach* that 'Philosophers have hitherto interpreted the world...; the task however is to change it.' Ideology involved not just an explanation of how the world worked but had to have a programme to change it as well. The programmatic part of Marx's theory was somewhat gradual and voluntaristic. Change occurred in his system slowly and independently of individual human agency. One could prepare the proletariat to struggle better, but one could not hasten history. In 1864, he founded the International Workingmen's Association, which was to educate workers in the class struggle and explain how the capitalists exploited them. Marx did not believe in an elite leadership, though he had little patience with his fellow socialists. The programmatic side of Communism is weak at this stage, while the theory of how society works and the reasons for its ills is strong. In Marx's work, Communism remains a philosophy – Marxism.

Marx's attempt to provide an action-oriented ideology was not successful, but his philosophy gained ground in the last third of the nineteenth century. A political party established in Germany, the German Social Democratic Workers Party, was the first party that claimed to be Marxist. Soon the growth of workers' movements in Europe led to the establishment of the second International Working-men's Association, better known as the Socialist International. The International remained, however, stronger in its rhetoric and limited in its actions. There were strikes, and in countries like Russia and in Eastern in Europe some desultory incendiary activity. The Communist as a bomb-thrower is a Russian type. It was from these incendiary origins that the Russian Social Democratic Labour Party arose. It was this party which was crucial to the conversion of Marxism from a philosophy to a full-scale ideology with a programme to change society. It was the leadership of Vladimir Ilyich Ulyanov – Lenin – which wrought this transformation.

Marx, however, had one ability which was very important in the spread of his ideas. He was a great stylist. His language could evoke storm and thunder and convey a vivid impression of impending conflict and crises. The very beginning of *The Communist Manifesto*, with its observation 'A Spectre Haunts Europe. It is the Spectre of Communism', brought the menace of Communism to life when Communists were a very small insignificant sect among many radical groups. Similarly, Marx's picture of the collapse of capitalism, when 'the expropriators will be expropriated' in the first volume of *Capital* was very evocative. While his theory was gradualist, his style made the oncoming collapse of capitalism seem imminent. This conflict between a gradualist theory and the imminent promise was reconciled by Lenin.

Lenin innovated the notion of a dedicated band of followers who would constitute the leadership of a vanguard party which would represent the proletariat, the main subject of historical change by means of their class struggle. Marx's theory of social change was converted into a theory of political action which would involve capturing the state and establishing a dictatorship of the proletariat. Lenin shared many of the characteristics that Savonarola and Calvin brought to their task – a single-minded belief in the rightness of his cause, a capacity to undertake immense hardship and inflict the same on others to realise his objective, and a complete indifference to the feelings of other people, who are seen only as puppets to be manipulated.

Lenin was more successful than any other ideologue of the previous two millennia. His Bolshevik Party succeeded in winning power in war-torn Russia in October–November 1917. Winning and then retaining power with remarkable ruthlessness, Lenin was able to consolidate Communism as an ideology. He had proven success on his side. He had the authority to mould Marx's philosophy into an ideology with a programmatic recipe to match the theory of how societies worked and how they could be changed. He established the Communist International whereby Communist Parties all over the world had to abide strictly by the tenets of what came to be called, after Lenin's death, Marxism–Leninism. These tenets required all Communist Parties to copy the dictatorial methods of the Bolshevik Party with its elite command structure and mindless obedience to the commands of the leadership. Communists were to lead dedicated, disciplined lives and be ready to undergo any sacrifice, perform any deed, for the sake of the Party. They were to eschew any reformist policies and discourage any relief of the problems the workers faced, as it could delay the final revolution. They were to prepare for a violent overthrow of the system wherever they operated.

Marx and Engels operated very much on their own. The International Workingmen's Association lasted only eight years, between 1864 and 1872. The party formed in Germany which claimed to adhere to Marxist principles found Marx and Engels wary of such an enterprise. Much of the time while they lived, Marx and Engels were engaged in non-violent activities of speech-making and pamphlet writing. They were suspected of regicide, of having fomented the Paris Commune uprising in 1871, and acquired a reputation for violent conduct. But they and their followers were on the margins of society and hunted by the police of many countries.

Polemical battles were frequent among Communists after the deaths of Marx and Engels. Karl Kautsky, a leading light of the German Social Democratic Party, began to fashion Marxism into an orthodoxy and appointed himself as final arbiter of what was and what was not Marxist. But until the Bolsheviks won power, these controversies were just verbal. Despite the rhetoric being violent, the comrades did not kill each other. Once power was won by the Bolsheviks, though, the rhetoric became truly lethal. Lenin began by using the tsarist secret police to his own purpose and fashioned a formidable instrument for terror to force dissidents to behave themselves. He saw this as essential for the survival of the revolution.

In the hands of his successor Josef Stalin, Communism became a truly terrorist ideology. The terror was unleashed as part of state action against dissidents within the USSR, especially against other Party members who were alleged to have deviated from the commands of the leadership. The Communist International (Comintern) also tried to instigate the violent overthrow of other governments through the use of the secretive Communist Parties. Communists everywhere had to adhere strictly to Party discipline and adapt themselves to drastic changes of directives as to the nature of the class enemy.

For the Comintern, the main enemy for Communists was not so much the capitalists or parties of the right but socialists, who often shared their admiration for Marx's ideas or at least the egalitarian vision of his philosophical writings. Even worse were people who had left the Communist Party to form new parties or factions. Thus when Hitler came to power in 1933, Stalin enjoined the German Communist Party to ignore the Nazis and concentrate its fire on the socialists, who were said to be the more dangerous. Ideology demanded purity of faith, and only the chosen ideologues were pure.

The reason why many Communists put up with this was that the promise was the end of all poverty and inequality, of exploitation, when Communism arrived. The future was what inspired immense sacrifices, and for the true believer it was a future worth killing for – or indeed, as happened more often, to be killed for. In power, the Communist Party was a ruthless terror machine deployed against its own members and citizens. Where not in power, the Communist Party was an instrument for clandestine struggle, taking orders from Moscow where the Communist International was based. The Party organised workers and planned sabotage of production where possible, and elimination of their rivals who were also on the left where feasible. Purges were frequent whereby members were eliminated, sometime literally.

Thus Communism had the complete makings of an ideology: a theory of history explaining how we had arrived at the present from the past. There had been a golden age of primitive Communism when complete equality prevailed. The present was degraded because of exploitation and class divisions between the rich and the poor. The answer was incessant class struggle led by the Communist Party, which was to bring about a revolution and thus the future – a Communist society would be brought nearer. When Communism arrives, it will be the end of the pre-history of mankind, Marx said. But to get there required many sacrifices, especially vigilance against the class enemy, who had to be ruthlessly eliminated. Violence was part and parcel of the ideology. The notion of class struggle may have been a perennial theme in Marx's theory of history, but in the hands of Lenin and Stalin it became a murderous doctrine. (The similarity with the Islamic notion of jihad is obvious and I will develop it later.) Much worse was to happen in Cambodia where, in the latter part of the 1970s, the Communist Khmer Rouge, while in power under the leadership of Pol Pot (Saloth Sar), killed two million people – roughly one-seventh of the total population. The idea was that since peasants were the dominant class in Cambodia, to create a classless society all other classes should be eliminated, literally.[23]

Yet Communism was able to recruit many idealistic young people across the world – in rich countries as in poor countries, from rich families as from poor families, educated and the illiterate. People were willing to betray their country, for example, by spying or supplying secrets because they believed the Soviet Union was in danger and needed help from everyone who subscribed to Communism. The famous Cambridge students who became spies, Burgess and Maclean, were part of the Establishment. They were not alienated in any ordinary sense of the term. In China, on the other hand, many students from middle-class rural and urban families joined the Communist Party and struggled against persecution by the Kuomintang government of Chiang Kai Sheik and the invading Japanese. They were defeated, but a rump was able to go on a Long March to establish a government in the Yenan mountains and eventually defeat the Japanese and the Kuomintang. This required immense dedication from a small band of core members. Ideology has the power to inspire such immense sacrifice, which defies any rational cost–benefit calculus. Similar stories can be told about Vietnam and Cuba, where Communists came to power, but also in India, Indonesia and Malaysia, where they were never in power.

Between Marxism as a philosophy and Communism as a state terrorist ideology there are many stages. The socialist movement which had been flourishing in Europe in the late nineteenth century split when the Bolshevik Revolution took place. The insistence on strict discipline and obedience to the dictates of the Communist International were disliked by many socialists. They remained socialist parties. If they adhered to a Marxist vision, believing in the eventual crisis and collapse of capitalism, they often called themselves 'democratic socialists'. This was because they hoped to come to power by democratic means. A milder version was the social-democratic one, which did not count on the eventual collapse of capitalism but did think it could be reformed and made more humane. The crucial difference between these parties and the Communist Party was that the latter believed in secretive methods rather than open democratic ones for coming to power. The Communists also banked on a violent overthrow of the existing order.

Violence and its absolute necessity were and remain Communist hallmarks.

However, eventually the Communist Soviet Union lost the Cold War and collapsed under the weight of its own problems of economic efficiency and the need to give people freedom. Along with the Soviet Union, Communism disappeared everywhere in Europe. In Western Europe, the many Communist Parties – in France, Italy, Great Britain – mutated or just died. But Marxist sects – Trotskyist, Maoist and so on – flourish on the fringes of politics. These sects use the vituperative violent language of the Bolsheviks, but they are harmless since they are never likely to be in power. They are also, by and large, non-violent, except for Maoist groups engaged in guerrilla warfare in Nepal and India, for example. Marxism continues to have a residual influence in Western politics, but Communism as a terrorist ideology has disappeared from Europe. It still survives in China, but howsoever repressive the Chinese Communist Party is of its own citizens, it does not try to foment revolution abroad as the Communist International did.

The story of Communism is thus that of an ideology which was capable of immense terrorism, and which did succeed for a few decades in doing just that. Yet it collapsed, and thus we need to learn how it was that this terrorist ideology was defeated. Also by analogy with Islamism, milder forms of the ideology continue to flourish, but the fangs are taken out of the most virulent variant of the doctrine.

An interesting example of the terrorist influence of Communism was seen in Western Europe and the USA in the 1960s and 1970s. The Vietnam War in which America was engaged, along with the Civil Rights struggle for American black people, revived left and revolutionary anarchist ideology. Student rebellion erupted across the two sides of the Atlantic. However it failed to move governments, though it came close to doing so in France in May 1968. In the aftermath of the ebbing of the rebellion, there were isolated groups that took to a harder type of violence. The Weathermen in America, the Baader–Meinhof Group, the Angry Brigade in Britain, the Red Army in Japan and the Red Brigades in Italy were all opposed to the established capitalist/bourgeois democratic system and wanted to destroy it. These movements succeeded in inflicting random violence – kidnapppings, murders, robberies, and so on, but eventually they were fought to a standstill and then defeated. Decentralised terrorist violence of this kind without state support does not typically last long.

The interesting thing about the 1960s' groups is that they were not state-supported, and operated very much in a decentralised fashion. Though their ideology was anti-capitalist and inspired by Marxism–Leninism, they behaved more like their anarchist predecessors. Terrorist violence was the innovation of nineteenth-century anarchists. A secretive, fanatical, urban, young male going about with his hat tipped down and a scarf around his face to hide his identity – the anarchist became a staple of horror stories that European monarchies and even republics fed themselves. Peter Marshall, a historian of anarchism, citing *Roget's Thesaurus*, said: 'The anarchist finds good company with the vandal, iconoclast, savage, brute, ruffian, hornet, viper, ogre, ghoul, wild beast, fiend, harpy and siren.' In this, the modern Islamist terrorist is a descendant of the anarchist, except that there is a central 'office', al-Qaeda, which either controls them or at least inspires them.

The anarchists had no such central office. By definition they would not tolerate such a central entity. Yet they had an ideology. Like other ideologies, anarchism had its peaceful side and its violent side, its philosophical/polemical side and its activist/organisational side. The anarchist had an abhorrence of central ruling authorities and indeed believed that the ills of the world stemmed from such centralising authority. As Pierre-Joseph Proudhon, a leading French philosopher of anarchism, wrote:

> To be governed is to be watched over, inspected, spied on, directed, legislated, regimented, closed in, indoctrinated, preached at, controlled, assessed, evaluated, censored, commanded; all by creatures that have neither the right, nor wisdom, nor virtue. To be governed means that at every move, operation, or transaction, one is noted, registered, entered in a census, taxed, stamped, priced, assessed, patented, licensed, authorised, recommended, admonished, prevented, reformed, set right, corrected. Government means to be subjected to tribute, trained, ransomed, exploited, monopolised, extorted, pressured, mystified, robbed; all in the name of public utility and the general good. Then at the first sign of resistance or word of complaint, one is repressed, fined, despised, vexed, pursued, hustled, beaten up, garrotted, imprisoned, shot, machine-gunned, judged, sentenced, deported, sacrificed, sold, betrayed, and to cap it all, ridiculed, mocked, outraged and dishonoured. *That* is government, *that* is its justice and its morality.[24]

At its philosophical best, in the hands of Rousseau or Godwin, anarchism is against the state itself and espouses the virtues of voluntary cooperation among free individuals. Individuals are capable of voluntary arrangements in a 'State of Nature'. This State of Nature is not violent and life is not, as Hobbes said in his *Leviathan* in the oft-quoted words, 'solitary, poor, nasty, brutish and short'. Life is benign and conflict-free. Indeed it is based on notions of mutuality and equality. It is only when the snake of order appears in the form of the state that equality is destroyed. The state monopolises force and creates hierarchies and conflict. States then go to war with each other – while societies do not.

Proudhon gave the ideology of anarchism an economic philosophy by questioning the sanctity of private property. 'Property is theft' is his best-known slogan. Proudhon gave anarchism a left, almost socialist colouring and made anarchism anti-capitalist. Here again one could contrast small self-employed craftsmen and large factories. Concentration and centralisation of economic power as an inevitable consequence of industrialisation and capitalism were opposed by anarchists. The only form of organisation they liked were trade unions or *syndicates*, which had to be fiercely anti-capitalist. Syndicalism, as the idea came to be called, wanted society to be organised by syndicates that would take over property from the capitalist in a violent overthrow of the state and of capitalism.

Marxists disagreed with the anarchists/syndicalists. Marx and the Russian anarchist Mikhael Bakunin had many quarrels during the proceedings of the First International Workingmen's Association. Bakunin was impatient for workers to overthrow the state, while Marx thought such an action would be premature. Marx believed in mass action but in the form of a disciplined well-organised and conscious working class. He was fascinated by the spontaneous uprising in France which led to the founding of the Paris Commune. Here was self-organisation of the citizens from the bottom up. But this was in the aftermath of the French defeat in the Franco-Prussian War and did not last long. But anarchists and Communists continued to fight about who should lead the workers.

Anarchism was popular in Russia in the second half of the nine-teenth century. In the form of a populist movement Narodnaya Volya (People's Will), anarchism became the first serious political movement in tsarist Russia to attract broad support from the edu-cated youth. These young people were willing to engage in violent activities; this culminated in the assassination of Tsar Alexander II himself in March 1881. Anarchism appealed to the young because while Marxism emphasised study and waiting for the development of productive forces until the time was ripe for a revolution, an-archists could at least throw bombs and hope to kill kings and presidents. President Garfield of the USA was another 'ruler' killed by anarchists. It was a philosophy of action. Gavrilo Princip was a Serbian nationalist who was member of a 'Black Hands' group dedicated to freeing Slavs from Austrian rule. It was he who killed Archduke Ferdinand and his wife Isabella when they were visiting Sarajevo in 1914. This led to the First World War. Nationalism and anarchism merged in his action.[25]

Yet, in principle, an adherent of the free market idea can also be an anti-state anarchist but not anti-capitalist. It is possible to adhere to an idea that private property in small amounts can be owned by self-employed people and their mutual interests would establish a peaceful but prosperous society relying on Adam Smith's famous 'invisible hand'. Such a society can be stateless and peaceful, at least in theory. There is a variant, libertarianism, that believes in the need for a minimal state. Either way, the phil-osophy is individualist and anti-authority. Henry David Thoreau is perhaps the most famous American anarchist. There has been an individualist anti-state tradition in American thinking since the origin of the Republic.

Sometimes the anarchist tradition in America takes a violent turn, as in the case of Timothy McVeigh, who destroyed an Oklahoma federal building in April 1995. He said he was defending the Constitution. There is a scattered anarchist right-wing movement in America which suspects either that the federal government has betrayed the Constitution by taking too much power to itself or that it has sold out American sovereignty to the United Nations, which now rules over the country and therefore must be destroyed. During the 1950s and 1960s there was a movement to impeach the Supreme Court Chief Justice Earl Warren, as well as groups such as the Minutemen who were armed and prepared for insurrection. The Ku Klux Klan is another anarchist terrorist outfit which has operated sporadically over much of the twentieth century in America. Such movements are also racist and white supremacist, but their roots are in an anti-state anarchism.

The ideology closest to Islamism is of course nationalism. As an ideology, nationalism originates at the turn of the nineteenth century. Its roots are in the Napoleonic wars, when Germany and other European territories were fighting Napoleon, and later in anti-imperial struggles, first in eastern and central Europe against the Austro-Hungarian and Ottoman empires. Irish nationalism is another strand within the British Isles. The colonial peoples of the British, French, Spanish and Dutch empires across Latin America, Africa and Asia also fought on an ideology of nationalism. Since a nation can be a primordial entity, or an 'imagined community', in Benedict Anderson's pithy expression, reconstructed in modern times with modern instruments of communication – the printing press, for example – nationalism is a mixture of the old and the new. The nation, whichever one it is, is seen as timeless and with a glorious past. But the nationalist finds his nation in chains because of the imperial power (later, after independence, in thrall to multinational capital or a neocolonial enemy). The nation has to struggle to realise its destiny. Independence is the beginning of redemption, often the climax of the struggle.

Nationalists as they fought the imperial power were obviously stateless and hence had to organise in a clandestine way. The anarchist was often fighting in his own country against tsar or kaiser. The colonial nationalist was fighting against a foreign, alien power. Thus he counted on the support of his own people, who shared his language, ethnicity, religion. Since the enemy was powerful and commanded troops, the nationalist resorted to sporadic violence. Sometimes there could be guerrilla warfare waged by the nationalist movement, as in the case of Zimbabwe or Bangladesh on their way to independence. Other times the struggle could be long drawn out, as in the case of the Irish nationalist movement which went on after the Settlement in 1922 to protest against the hiving off of the six counties of Ulster. This struggle lasted through the twentieth century, carried out at first by the Irish Republican Army (IRA) and later, after 1968, by the Provisional IRA. The Jewish nationalist movement in Palestine before the Second World War formed a group, the Irgun, which was for the Jews a liberation army and for the occupying British forces a terrorist group. It continued bombing and other attacks after 1945, and indeed until the formation of the State of Israel in 1948. In classic style, like many other leaders of violent anti-colonial movements who were denounced as terrorists by their foreign masters, Menachem Begin, who was a member of the Irgun, became prime minister of Israel later in his life.

Outside Europe, nationalism became anti-Western and often anti-capitalist as well, especially after the Bolshevik Revolution of 1917. It borrowed from the Communist ideology as well as from anarchism. But once independence had been gained, nationalists wanted a powerful centralised state, not an anarchist collective of decentralised communities. Prior to the gaining of independence, nationalists had to be secretive and conspiratorial. Until Mahatma (Mohandas) Gandhi came and waged an open non-violent mass struggle for Indian independence, there was a terrorist strand in India, Anushilan. It inspired many young men, mainly Bengali Hindus, to undertake violent activities against the British. Later there were other martyrs who, in anarchist fashion, tried to assassinate or blow up British targets. They were (and indeed are) heroes for the Indians, but were hanged or sent into exile by the British rulers. The Black Hands group to which Gavrilo Princip belonged was such an outfit, committed to Slav independence from the Habsburgs. Terrorism was their weapon, but as it was deployed in a nationalist cause after independence the terrorists are celebrated as martyrs. The terrorist/martyr if he dies or the terrorist/leader if he survives until independence is equally a familiar figure in modern history. Nelson Mandela is the most famous example of this type, who was denounced as a terrorist by the apartheid regime, and indeed by British prime minister Margaret Thatcher, but lived on to become a statesman of world stature.

The empires of Europe disappeared in two waves. First, after the end of the First World War, the land-based empires of Austria–Hungary and the Ottomans broke up, though (as we saw above) their after-effects are still with us. The Romanov Empire of the tsars was taken over by the Bolsheviks, and indeed expanded after the Second World War through their formal and informal control over eastern Europe. The maritime empires of Britain, France and Netherlands dissolved after the Second World War. Of course, there was a lengthy struggle in Algeria and Indochina where the French ruled. There was also guerrilla war in Malaya waged by Communists, violent struggle in Kenya where the Mau Mau fought the British and in Zimbabwe. The empire of Portugal in Angola and Mozambique witnessed scenes of bloody struggle, and, following decolonisation, of civil war. In all these cases, the nationalists resorted to terrorist tactics both at home and in the metropolitan mainland.

A distinctive feature of the late twentieth century is liberation struggles against Big Powers, who were not the original foreign rulers but invited by the local rulers to defend them. The USA got involved in a long, bloody and finally humiliating war in Vietnam under the pretext of stopping the spread of Communism. For fifteen years from 1960 to 1975, America tore itself apart as it played an imperial role shoring up a corrupt regime in South Vietnam, while claiming to fight for freedom. The Soviet Union did the same in Afghanistan, and was similarly humiliated. The lesson that many liberation movements learnt from these episodes was that the Big Powers were militarily vulnerable. Osama Bin Laden definitely took inspiration from these examples.

As an ideology, nationalism lacks the structure that Marxism–Leninism or even anarchism has. This is because the future is realised as soon as the nation becomes a nation-state. There may remain territorial disputes, since the nation may not be all in one territory, as happened in the case of Ireland. But in most cases the past is a distant time when the nation was free. The present is foreign rule and the future is independence. Each nation has its own variation on the story. The common thread is that a violent struggle has to be waged, if the foreign ruler is to be ousted. Terrorist acts – bombings, kidnappings, assassinations – are all admissible for the nationalist. Of course, once the nation becomes a nation-state such acts become prohibited. Often, sub-nationalisms emerge from the sentiments of minorities, who see themselves as not part of the ur-nation or as disadvantaged in the division of spoils after independence. Then the struggle resumes within the nation-state. Bangladesh's move for independence from Pakistan, and the ongoing Tamil Tigers war against the Sri Lankan Sinhala majority are examples of such struggles. There is a long-running struggle for Basque independence waged by ETA (Euskadi Ta Askatasuna), which has led to terrorism charges against its leaders. Chechnya's struggle against Russia is another such quarrel, which has been taken by the Chechnyans to the Russian heartland. For the nation-state, often recently independent, these movements are terrorist ones waged by traitors. For the fighters, they are liberation struggles.

In the case of the Tamil Tigers, the Sri Lankan Tamil diaspora has been a great source of finance. Globalisation has made such flows of money, and often drugs and arms, easier to deliver than was the case thirty years ago. Similar stories can be told about the Palestine Liberation Organisation or the Khalistan movement which struggled for an independent nation for Sikhs in India. Thus local struggles acquire international linkages, and again terrorism can spread far away from the base.

A nation is, thankfully for the nationalist, not a simple concrete thing with determined borders, a birth date and a recorded life.

Nations can be conjured up as long as some basis for a common element in culture, language or religion can be found. One can divide a nation into sub-nations, each claiming a separate identity, and one can combine nations into a super-nation. It was fashionable at the beginning of the twentieth century to imagine Africa as a single nation fighting Western imperialism. The Pan-African Movement raised the banner of black liberation and inspired in its turn the American Black Liberation Movement. The Pan-Africanists argued that Western imperialism had artificially divided Africa into separate territories, whereas Africa was a unity and shall be so again once the imperialists have been removed. But since the Empires dissolved, Africa has found itself divided into separate nation-states jealous of their boundaries. When the Organisation for African Unity was set up, one of its early resolves was that existing boundaries, even though drawn by the foreign rulers, were to be respected as valid and not challenged.

Arabia is a similar imaginary nation, which still has some emotional appeal to Muslims of the Middle East (though there are many non-Muslim Arabs). In analogy with Africa, a story could be constructed of Arabia's suffering as having been caused by the imperialist West. This has the advantage of appealing to a large Arab population which is currently divided into separate nations and kingdoms. To give Arab nationalism an ideology had been attempted by secular forces such as the Ba'ath Party, but secular nationalism proved inadequate to the task. It is now the turn of the Islamists to try again. Since many of the national Islamist parties are concerned with the capture of power within the national context, it has fallen to the Global Islamists to take up the challenge. But of course they use the appeal of religion, especially the notion of the *umma*, to unify the Arabs. Yet nationalists also need an enemy, an Other to be able to rail against as a unifying factor. It is here that Israel and the United States serve their function as the Other, the Enemy whose presence keeps the 'Arab Nation' in thrall. It is as a response to this 'crisis' that Global Islamism has been propagated.

Conclusion

There have always been religions that have formed the bases of reform programmes and political movements. Buddha and Jesus launched reform movements with a religious message. So did Muhammad as he tried to cleanse what he regarded as darkness – *jahiliya* – in his days. In Europe, the schism between Protestants and Catholics led to religious wars and much change. It was as a result of the rational approach to the study of the Bible that Luther inaugurated what led to an intellectual, rational attitude towards religion. One consequence was to lead to the Enlightenment, which encouraged a purely secular approach to human problems. For two hundred years, a separation of Church and State became the mark of modernity, at least in Protestant countries. Religion was a part of the private sphere and not a matter for the state. Ideology became secular as well. Marxism became the most powerful ideology of the twentieth century because it offered a millenarian hope and a programme to achieve it. Other ideologies – anarchism, nationalism, Nazism – also flourished as programmatic devices for liberation or for restoration of national pride.

Religion did not quite disappear from the field of social reform however. In Latin America, liberation theology was a strong movement which involved the Church in reform programmes, often in defiance of the state. The Catholic Church maintained an active social profile partly as a counter to Communism but also to respond to the expectations of its followers for an answer to the myriad social problems they had. Religion became a social but unofficial activity as it took part in reform. What distinguishes Islamism from such efforts is that it is a political ideology with a programme which is explicitly related to power relations. It is this which has surprised many people who mistake it for a religion seeking political power. I take this up in the next chapter.

FOUR

The Ideology of Global Islamism

'I have always dreamed of a band of men absolute in
their resolve to discard all scruples in the choice of
means, strong enough to give themselves frankly the
name of destroyers, and free from the taint of that
resigned pessimism which rots the world. No pity for
anything on earth, including themselves – and death
– enlisted for good and all in the service of humanity
– that's what I would like to see.'

(The anarchist Karl Yundt,
in Joseph Conrad, *The Secret Agent*)

The Attack on the Twin Towers

The attack on the Twin Towers in New York was innovative in
many ways. It was a well-planned and sophisticated instance of
guerrilla warfare, conducted far away from base, on enemy territory, with simple weapons which were leveraged into weapons of
mass destruction. It may have been denounced as senseless, and, as

often happens in such cases, as cowardly. But it had a logic and a supporting ideology which did not make it an accident or a random event. Well-educated and indeed foreign-trained middle-class men gave up lucrative careers and a promising future to sacrifice all in what they knew to be a suicidal act. Cowards run away from battle; they do not embrace it. And they were not alone; nor was their attack an isolated incident.

The abhorrence that the attack inspired in many people in the West but perhaps also around the world must not cloud our judgement. One may hate the terrorists but one should also try to understand their motivation and the logic behind their act. The attack on the Twin Towers, coming as it did at the end of several earlier events all directed against the USA, invites us to place it in the global context of American policy in the post-Cold War era. It is the twin effects of globalisation and the emergence of the USA as the sole superpower, a hyper-power as the French have described it, which makes the attack a piece of global guerrilla war waged by a small but clever organisation that also has benefited from the modern developments in means of transport and communications as well as management techniques.

Al-Qaeda has been studied and mapped in great detail and we do not need to add to those studies here.[26] It is a small but efficient outfit which has decentralised or franchised (without any fee of course) its operations and is thus a 'flat' corporation much in line with modern management doctrine. Many groups claim to be part of al-Qaeda but often just use the name as a brand or a logo. Bin Laden could hardly object as it enhances his reputation for omnipresence. Even his enemies see the hand of al-Qaeda behind every bombing outrage. Al-Qaeda is the most successful brand, even though its business is terror. While it started in the context of a national liberation struggle in Afghanistan, it found itself in new circumstances when that battle was won. It responded to these new circumstances in an imaginative way. These circumstances were created by several events.

The Historical Background

First was the collapse of the Soviet Union. Whatever its short-comings, the Soviet Union represented an alternative to the liberal/capitalist model, epitomised by the USA and its allies, especially the UK. All those people who for one reason or another did not like the policies, the culture or the societies of the Western liberal capitalist democracies (diverse though they are) could always look to the USSR for hope of an alternative. After the Second World War, Communist regimes had proliferated all over Asia, Africa and Latin America as well as Europe. Cuba, Ethiopia, Cambodia, Vietnam, the Korean Democratic Republic plus China gave people the hope that another society was possible. The Soviet Union also helped, given its limited resources, with arms and cash and equipment those regimes that wanted to defy the World Bank or IMF or the NATO countries. The disappearence of the USSR was an unprecedented event, since it fell without a defeat in a war or an internal rebellion. Its worst enemies on the American right had demonised it as the Great Satan but did not imagine that it could fall apart so quickly. (Though they did in retrospect claim credit for Ronald Reagan and his aggressive stance for having achieved this goal.) Their detractors on the left – the myriad Trotskyist factions – were predicting an uprising by the working class of the

USSR to correct the mistakes of the original revolution. When the Soviet Union collapsed, the working class hardly raised a finger at home or abroad.

The Eastern European satellites of the USSR gave up their old arrangements with an alacrity and a vengeance that was shocking. Many people in the Third World had convinced themselves that, despite all the Western propaganda, the citizens of socialist Eastern Europe were creating an alternative social order. Shockingly, they found that the Western propagandists were right all along, and that the socialism was sham. The Wizard of Oz was not a great ogre, nor someone who could be a benevolent giver. He was a sad old man exaggerating his strength. What many thought was the future was found to be obsolete.

By the early 1990s, when these events took place, the world economy had been through a tough two decades beginning with the oil shock of 1973. Inflation and unemployment in the developed countries and debt crises in the developing countries of Latin America and Africa had led to severe difficulties. The IMF had moved in with its structural adjustment programmes, which countries in economic difficulties had to sign up to. Public budgets were slashed and any subsidies to the poor had to be cut. Life became hard for many countries, and the alternative of rejecting capitalism was no longer available. Many states failed and became anarchic– Sierra Leone, Somalia, Liberia, Zaire. Yugoslavia fell apart with ethnic cleansing in the backyard of Europe. States which used to be part of the old USSR and were now independent saw their economies collapse, and their rulers indulge in the most rapacious looting of public assets. Many of these states had a large Muslim population which had thus far been subjected to religious repression. Now that the old system could no longer provide bread or circuses, the time was ripe for Islamists to move in.

Globalisation accelerated the spread of liberal capitalism. Many countries that had sought to use their independence to fashion a national development strategy found that they were exposed to the vagaries of the international bond markets. They had lost their economic sovereignty. Countries that had a more or less well-functioning economy found that with the increased availability of private capital old policies did not work any longer. Mexico had followed the advice of the IMF and won praise for its policy. When the peso collapsed in December 1993, there was widespread misery. The Zapatistas chose this moment to show their rejection of the Mexican political system, since they had been left out of any benefits while bearing all the costs. Asian banks received a large inflow of portfolio capital during the mid-1990s, but could not handle such flows. Money flowed out more rapidly than it had flowed in. The Asian crisis of 1997 hit Malaysia, Indonesia, Thailand and South Korea. It then spread to Turkey and Russia in 1998. Large numbers of Muslims in Asia, Turkey and Russia were ruined by these happenings. While there was a quick recovery in South Korea, in Malaysia and Indonesia it was a long time before income and employment recovered.[27]

Rightly or not, people saw in globalisation the power of America, of its multinationals and of the IMF, which they took to be a tool of American policy.[28] They saw US presidents and politicians preaching the message that free movements of capital and free trade were going to bring prosperity to all. So they held America responsible for globalisation. America itself was conscious that, as the sole super-power, it had to construct and police the 'New World Order'. Its intervention in Somalia, where there was a serious humanitarian crisis, cost the Americans precious lives. There was a dawning realisation that the post-Cold War world was more anarchic than when the two powers had their 'spheres of influence' to keep in order. People began to criticise America for intervening, but also for not intervening – as in the case of Rwanda. In Yugoslavia, the break-up saw ineffectual European intervention. Again Muslims were slaughtered in ethnic cleansing by Christians, who of course were also slaughtering each other if they belonged to Catholic or Orthodox sects. America had to step in to provide air cover before the crisis was resolved. The Yugoslav crisis caused much more distress in the Muslim world than Europeans could imagine.

In a sense, the ordered world of the Cold War days had slid into a neo-medieval state. The UN damaged its reputation by letting Rwanda suffer one of the worst genocides of modern times and by being unable to influence the crisis in Somalia, Sudan, Ethiopia and later Zaire. The Americans also threw their weight around in the UN, not paying their dues and insisting on sacking Boutros-Ghali, its secretary-general. When Clinton bombed Afghanistan in the wake of the bombing of the American embassy in Nairobi, many saw it as a cynical ploy to divert attention from his own personal difficulties about Monica Lewinsky.

The Evil Genius of Osama Bin Laden

The missiles that were launched against Afghanistan were meant to kill Osama Bin Laden, who by this time had emerged as the face of al-Qaeda.[29] As usual, they missed him. Osama Bin Laden had transformed himself from a rich man volunteering to fight against the Soviet soldiers in Afghanistan into a central figure in recruiting, training and deploying young Muslim volunteers – mujahideen – to fight in wars around the world where Muslims were involved as victims. He saw the logic of globalisation, of thinking globally and acting locally. He sensed that with the new facilities for rapid transport and communication, he could deploy his volunteers around the world with a small central office. Guerrilla warfare had been practised even before the Spanish resistance to Napoleon gave the tactic its name. In Vietnam, General Nguyen von Giap had perfected the tactic, and defeated the mighty army of the USA. Che Guevara was perhaps less successful in his guerrilla campaigns, and failed to foment a revolution in Bolivia. Yet he had the same ideas. Guerrilla warfare relied on local support in which the warrior could disappear into the civilian population and reappear to fight the enemy at will. Guerrillas had to be lightly equipped, mobile and flexible. The command structure also had to be light rather than top-heavy, since it had to improvise.

Osama Bin Laden adapted this tactic to global circumstances. In urban areas around the world, but especially in metropolitan areas of America and Europe, it was easy for a warrior to be anonymous. Not only was there a large diaspora of Muslims, but all big cities are racially mixed. A Muslim is not racially distinct from people of many other nationalities since Islam spread across all continents. Big cities also provide many facilities for a newcomer to live and spend money and time. There are credit cards and ATMs, airlines open to quick reservations and equally to quick changes of plan. There are facilities for faking identities, places to rent at short notice which provide safe houses in which to hide. Modern life has abolished neighbourhoods in large cities, and people barely know

THE IDEOLOGY OF GLOBAL ISLAMISM 95

or care who lives in their apartment building or down their street. People may not like it, but they do not pry into the lifestyles of their neighbours. Thus the environment is perfect for the guerrilla. While in Vietnam and in Che Guevara's last campaigns in Latin America, jungles and mountains were used for cover, now the urban landscape provided the best cover.

Sinister though he may be, Bin Laden has to be seen as a military genius of global guerrilla warfare. The forces deployed against him, as was seen during Clinton's missile launches on Afghanistan, are, by comparison, top-heavy and clumsy. During January 2006, there was a flurry of excitement that Ayman al-Zawahiri, Bin Laden's deputy, had been killed in the mountains on border of Afghanistan and Pakistan. Yet again missiles were used and while some people died – ordinary villagers as well as alleged al-Qaeda members – the main target escaped.

However, much more than his military prowess, it is in the fashioning of ideology of Global Islamism that one must study Osama Bin Laden's ideas. Calling him a terrorist is not the end of the matter. He is a much more serious figure than say a George Habash or a Carlos the Jackal. His achievement has been to take a number of themes which have been around in the Muslim discourse about modernity for a century and more and weave them into a global ideology. He also shows a knowledge of older debates about the nature of religion and of authority, of the proper behaviour of rulers and of the faithful. His speeches are full of allusions to these old debates and scholars of bygone ages. While he often addresses the West, he knows that his main target is the Muslim world, and thus his allusions and Qur'anic quotations have a larger impact than we realise. I shall be using his many speeches and the statements he has issued on the Internet extensively to construct the anatomy of the ideology of Global Islamism. He is in this way a serious interlocutor about the nature of the Muslim predicament in the late twentieth and early twenty-first centuries.

There have been many attempts to belittle Osama Bin Laden or accuse him of inconsistency or of changing his agenda. Thus people think that he was a creature of the CIA when he was fighting in Afghanistan. He denied this in an interview with Al-Jazeera the Arab television channel in December 1998.[30] This turns out to be true, since the CIA worked through the ISI of Pakistan, with which Bin Laden had few dealings. People have also accused him of mentioning Palestine only recently in his speeches to get on the right side of the most potent issue for Muslims around the world. But, again, a careful examination of his speeches shows this not to be the case. Bin Laden's very first public statement, an open letter to the Chief Mufti of Saudi Arabia in December 1994, concerns 'the betrayal of Palestine', as the English version of the letter's title indicates. Again, just because we do not approve of terrorism, it does not help to belittle the one person who has inspired many terrorists. It is better to understand what he is saying and why. This is what I intend to do. This is important because if the ideology constructed by Osama Bin Laden has any power, then he is dispensable as a person. Others will take up and develop the ideology and act upon it. So what is this ideology, what is Global Islamism?[31]

What is Global Islamism?

Global Islamism is the ideology that has waged a terrorist war on a global scale since the early 1990s. Al-Qaeda is its principal agency and Osama Bin Laden its leading figure. It is essential, in my view, to separate an analysis of Global Islamism from Islam as a religion but also from national and local manifestations of Political Islamism. Thus the victory of Hamas (Harakat al-Muqawamah al-Islamiya) in the Palestinian elections of January 2006 are an instance of Political Islamism where a terrorist organisation has become a democratically elected one. This is not as unique as is being argued, since the IRA has a political arm, Sinn Fein, which fought elections. Officially the Provisional IRA and Sinn Fein pretended that they were separate organisations, but it fooled no one. Hamas contested the elections under a reform banner and has not so far made a formal split between its military and its political arms. Yet there have been many other liberation movements, ZANU for example, which swung between violent struggle and democratic participation.

Global Islamism confronts the entire world, both Western and Eastern, North and South. Its terrorist activities have covered the USA, the UK, Spain, India, Indonesia, Kenya, Egypt, Saudi Arabia and Jordan. Its rhetoric is of a worldwide struggle against the Judeo-Christian 'Crusader' regimes, yet its victims have been Muslims, Hindus, Christians and Jews and all other religious communities. Yet its vision is a call to Muslims to defend their community, their *umma*. It recalls previous crises in the history of Islam when there were appeals by learned men to the community as to how to meet the challenge. Its rhetoric is meant to be heard or read by Muslims since there are allusions to the Qur'an and the traditions (*hadith*) of the Prophet, to historic events which every Muslim will know about such as the *hijra* (migration) of the Prophet from Mecca to Medina. There are references to the first four caliphs, who have, as we saw above, a special status.

The Saudi Outrage

At the start of Osama Bin Laden's discourse about the crisis in Islam is his complaint about the royal family of the Saud. The complaints are twofold. One is that they allow banking along normal commercial lines and hence encourage usury which is against the teachings of the Qur'an. Thus in the letter to the Grand Mufti, Osama says,

> We have heard from you only to the effect that practising usury is absolutely prohibited, although this position ignores the fact that your words deceive people because you do not distinguish in your judgment between those who merely practise usury and those who legitimise it and make it legal. In fact, the distinction between these two issues is very clear: he who practises usury is committing a serious and grave offence – but as for he who makes usury legal, in doing so he becomes an apostate and an infidel who has placed himself outside the religious community, because he has considered himself an equal and a partner to God in deciding what is permissible and what is not. (1994: 6–7)

To accuse the Saudi kings of apostasy is the strongest criticism one could make, especially since they are the guardians of the Holy places. Osama drives the point home by quoting the Prophet as having said 'There are 73 easier ways to offend God than usury, such as to marry your own mother.' But the charge of usury is compounded by the more serious one of allowing the stationing of foreign troops on the soil of the holy lands. Thus again Bin Laden chides the Mufti for defending the decision by issuing a fatwa in its favour.

> When the aggressive Crusader–Jewish alliance decided during the Gulf War – in connivance with the regime – to occupy the country in the name of liberating Kuwait, you justified it with an arbitrary

judicial decree excusing this terrible act, which insulted the pride of our *umma* and sullied its honour, as well as polluting its holy places. (6–7)

This is in fact the principal complaint Osama Bin Laden has against the Saudis and the Americans: that the holy land of Islam has been sullied by the presence of infidel troops. This is for him the most critical event in the twentieth century, if not the entire history of the Muslim *umma*. His anger against the Americans begins with this event. What was a sore spot in the history of the Muslims – the decline since the fall of the Ottoman Empire – has now been opened wider and allowed to fester by the presence of foreign troops. While this festering sore exists, the *umma* stays insulted and polluted.

It is hard to exaggerate the importance of this point in the Global Islamist ideology. To those in the West it may seem strange that so much fuss is made of the presence of foreign troops. After all, the host government approved of it; indeed, it invited the Americans to come and defend them. In western Europe, in the UK and Germany there are still American troops stationed, as they are in South Korea after fifty years. Foreign troops ran over much of Arabia when the Mongols invaded the region in the thirteenth century and conquered Iran and Iraq and a non-Muslim Mongol dynasty ruled for eighty years (1256–1336), though it did convert to Islam during its rule. During the First World War, Ottoman troops lost many battles against the British and French troops who occupied Syria and Iraq and captured Jerusalem. Thus, in a way, Osama exaggerates the uniqueness of the situation, but the power of his objection is in connecting the presence of these non-Muslim foreign troops, even with the permission of the royal family, to single out the insult to the holy land, the *hijaz*. By connecting the presence of the foreign troops to the insult of the *umma* as a whole, he delocalises the quarrel. It is not just a matter for the people who live in Saudi Arabia; it is a matter for Muslims everywhere. Osama drives this home by often exaggerating how much of the holy land the American troops occupy. Thus he says:

> The enemy invaded the land of our *umma*, violated her honour, shed her blood, and occupied her sanctuaries.
>
> This aggression has reached such a catastrophic and disastrous point as to have brought about a calamity unprecedented in the history of our *umma*, namely the invasion by the American and western Crusader forces of the Arabian peninsula and Saudi Arabia, the home of the Noble Ka'ba, the Sacred House of God, the Muslim's direction of prayer, the Noble Sanctuary of the Prophet and the city of God's Messenger, where the Prophetic revelation was received. (1995: 15–16)

Muslims will know that by 'the city of God's Messenger', Osama means Medina; the direction of prayer refers to Mecca. Of course the American troops are not in Mecca or Medina. But just as Marx and Engels thundered about the spectre of Communism, when in 1848 no such spectre existed, Osama gets a lot of effect by his alarmist rhetoric. The frequent references to the Prophet and the Ka'ba and the Sanctuary are designed to shock a Muslim, wherever he or she is. In the same letter, he repeats:

> And is there any torment – in the world, in the spirit, or the senses – worse for any believer than the humiliation and weakness that his *umma* is experiencing, not to mention the defilement of her holy places, occupation of her land, and violation and plundering of her sanctuaries?' (1995: 18)

No sanctuaries have been plundered and Muslim pilgrims going on the hajj were unlikely to see an American soldier. They certainly do not sense any defilement of the holy places as they continue to go there year on year. Still, the dramatic rhetoric is effective as it is heard by Muslim young men and women around the world.

Broadening the Reach

Soon Osama Bin Laden began to broaden his appeal to Muslims by referring to other battles and other struggles. He could thus weave a global appeal adding to the complaint about the occupation of the holy places, matters closer to other Muslims' concern. In 1996, he published 'A Letter from Sheikh Osama bin Muhammad Bin Laden to his Muslim Brothers across the world, and particularly those in the Arabian peninsula'. Above the main text is the slogan: 'Expel the Polytheists from the Arabian Peninsula'. After this start, he lays out what is the generic statement of Muslim humiliation, weaving the many local struggles into a single rhetorical cloth.

> It is no secret to you, my brothers, that the people of Islam have been afflicted with oppression, hostility, and injustice by the Judeo-Christian alliance and its supporters. This shows our enemies' belief that Muslims' blood is the cheapest and that their property and wealth is merely loot. Your blood has been spilt in Palestine and Iraq, and the horrific image of the massacre in Qana in Lebanon are still fresh in people's minds. The massacres that have taken place in Tajikistan, Burma, Kashmir, Assam, the Philippines, Fatani, Ogaden, Somalia, Eritrea, Chechnya, and Bosnia-Herzegovina send shivers down our spines and stir our passions. All this has happened before the eyes and ears of the world, but the blatant imperial arrogance of America, under the cover of the United Nations, has prevented the dispossessed from arming themselves. (1996: 25)

This is a vital piece in the construction of the ideology. It has echoes for Muslims, since the Israeli attack on a UN compound in Qana in Lebanon which killed 102 civilian refugees and injured many others is mentioned separately. The last sentence will also be read as referring to Palestinians as 'the dispossessed'. But also a whole list of locations around the world is made to show the global reach of the Muslim's plight. At the same time, the blame is put on the single agent, the Judeo-Crusader or the Judeo-Christian alliance. Of course, there are minor details Bin Laden ignores, such as the fact that Iraq had invaded a fellow Muslim country, Kuwait, and the world had gone to Kuwait's aid in the Gulf War of 1991–92. He does not also mention that one of the bloodiest battles in which a lot of Muslim blood was spilt was the eight year war between Iran and Iraq. Yet his purpose is not to write a factual history but to construct an ideology taking such facts as suit his purpose. In the sentence following the passage quoted above, Osama says: 'So the people of Islam realized that they were the fundamental target of the hostility of the Judeo-Crusader alliance.'

Marx and Engels in their *Manifesto* gave the world the slogan 'Workers of the World Unite'. They created the concept of a world-wide workers' alliance when, apart from England, few countries had a large industrial working class, even in Europe. At that time, capitalism had barely touched Western Europe, and the rest of the world was in various pre-capitalist modes. But by the rhetoric of asserting the existence of workers of the world, they created something which became real later, largely as a result of material developments but also partly as a result of their own conceptualising. Communism was always an internationalist programme, even as the Comintern sacrificed other Communist

Parties to the interests of the Soviet Union. Communism had a global reach because of the initial bold conceptualising by Marx and Engels. Bin Laden uses similar techniques. When Osama says 'the people of Islam realized', he means 'do realize, since you may not have thought about it this way, you Muslims'. He creates the category of people of Islam as part of his ideology since it is to appeal to them. Whether he succeeds or not is still to be decided, but he plants the seed of the thought that Muslims everywhere have a grievance against the West.

This letter also provides the first programmatic statement that Osama Bin Laden proposes. He uses religious texts and symbols to make his point, but the message is clear – fight against the enemy. He does this in a dramatic invocation of the Prophet's most famous struggle when he had withdrawn to Medina from Mecca. Appealing to 'the youth of Islam', Bin Laden says:

> I remind them of what Gabriel said to the Prophet after the battle of Ahzab: 'When the Messenger of God, prayers and peace be upon him, departed to Medina and laid down his sword, Gabriel came to him and said : – You have laid down your sword? By God, the angels have not yet laid down their swords. Get up and go with whoever is with you to the Bani Qurayza, and I will go ahead of you to shake their fortresses and strike fear into them – So Gabriel went off, accompanied by his pageant of angels, the Prophet and his holy warriors and helpers. (29–30)

Again, for a Muslim reader this is a very evocative quotation. The reference to Muhammad's retreat from Mecca (*hijra*) to Medina and his subsequent triumphant return to Mecca recalls central events in the history of Islam. Every Muslim would know them. Gabriel is the angel who first commanded Muhammad to read what God was about to reveal to him. Now it is Osama who is Gabriel, and the

Muslim youth has to emulate the Prophet and not despair. What is required is martyrdom. So he quotes:

> He will not let the deeds of those who are killed for his Cause come to nothing. He will guide them and put them in a good state; He will admit them into the Garden He has already made known to them. (Qur'an 47: 4–6)

In an interview with an Australian Muslim magazine Bin Laden made his message more explicit, by saying, 'terrorizing the American occupiers is a religious and logical obligation' (1996: 39).

Bin Laden was more articulate on this theme in a CNN interview with Peter Arnett. When asked why he had declared jihad against the Americans, and was it just against the government, against soldiers or against all Americans, his reply was very candid and thorough. He starts by putting his case against the US government:

> We declared jihad against the US government, because the US government is unjust, criminal, and tyrannical. It has committed acts that are extremely unjust, hideous, and criminal, whether directly or through its support of the Israeli occupation of the Land of the Prophet's Night Journey [Jerusalem]. And we believe the US is directly responsible for those who were killed in Palestine, Lebanon, and Iraq. The mention of the US reminds us before everything else of those innocent children who were dismembered, their heads and arms cut off in the recent explosion that took place in Qana [in Lebanon]. (1997: 46–7)

This style of denunciation is one that will have resonance among Muslims. Thus the reference to the Prophet's Night Journey will remind Muslims of the tradition in Islam that believes Muhammad was brought from Mecca to Jerusalem before he ascended to heaven from where after communing with many angels he returned to earth. If he had merely said Jerusalem, it would not have the same effect. But then, towards the end of a long answer, Bin Laden comes to the issue of American civilians:

> As for what you asked regarding the American people, they are not exonerated from responsibility, because they chose this government and voted for it despite their knowledge of its crime in Palestine, Lebanon, Iraq, and in other places, and its support of its client regimes who filled their prisons with our best children and scholars. (46–7)

This is not just against the Clinton presidency but against all American governments, indeed against the American state, since he mentions events which happened before Clinton took office in 1993. He comes back to this theme a little later in the interview. He mentions how the demise of the USSR made the US 'more haughty and arrogant' and how 'it has started to see itself as a Master of this world'. He adds:

> The US today, as a result of this arrogance, has set a double stand-ard, calling whoever goes against its injustice a terrorist. It wants to occupy our countries, steal our resources, install collaborators to rule us with man-made laws, and wants us to agree on all these issues. If we refuse to do so, we are terrorists... At the same time that they condemn any Muslim who calls for his rights, they receive the highest official of the Irish Republican Army [Gerry Adams] at the White House as a political leader, while woe, all woe if the Muslims cry out for their rights. (51)

The mention of the IRA and of Gerry Adams is telling, since it points to the obvious double standards being practised by the American presidency at that time. Even the British government, a loyal US ally, was chafing against the welcome accorded to IRA leaders at the time when the St Patrick's Day Parade was celebrated in New York and Boston. Perhaps the most astonishing thing in this interview is Bin Laden's explicit warning that he will take the fight to the US mainland. Peter Arnett asked him about Ramzi Yousef, who was convicted for bombing the World Trade Center. After denying that he knows Ramzi Yousef, Osama says:

> But I say if the American government is serious about avoiding explosion inside the US, then let it stop provoking the feelings of 1.25 billion Muslims. Those hundreds of thousands who have been killed or displaced in Iraq, Palestine, and Lebanon, do have brothers and relatives [who] will make of Ramzi Yousef a symbol and a teacher. The US will drive them to transfer the battle into the United States. Everything is made possible to protect the blood of the American citizen while the bloodshed of Muslims is permitted everywhere. With this kind of behavior, the US government is hurting itself, hurting Muslims and hurting the American people. (53)

Here again, Osama makes himself the representative of 1.25 billion Muslims, the majority of whom live far from Arabia. Many live in the USA and in Europe and may not agree with him in his views. Yet his general political critique is not novel; we encounter it in the writings of Edward Said or Noam Chomsky, for instance. The inconsistencies in American policies as between Israel and the Muslim Middle East are well documented. The welcome given to the IRA by the American president while the British government was trying to fight terrorism in Northern Ireland even struck Conservative prime ministers in Britain as peculiar. It was only after 9/11 that the American government made the IRA suffer the same boycott as other terrorist groups, though one has to wonder if a Democratic president with a large stake in Massachussets votes would have been as quick as George W. Bush was.

In 1998, Bin Laden launched the World Islamic Front along with Ayman al-Zawahiri as well as leaders from Egypt, Pakistan and Bangladesh. In its declaration was this statement:

> To kill Americans and their allies-civilians and military – is an individual duty incumbent upon every Muslim in all countries, in order to liberate the al-Aqsa Mosque [in Jerusalem] and the Holy Mosque [in Mecca] from their grip, so that their armies leave all the territory of Islam, defeated, broken, and unable to threaten any Muslim. (1998: 61)

Here again the reference to 'all the territory of Islam' separates Arabia (including Palestine) from every other land where Muslims live and gives it special status. This is an ideological ploy because after all Muslims can go to both of the mosques and millions of hajj pilgrims do go to Mecca every year. There is no need to 'liberate' the Holy Mosque or the Al-Aqsa Mosque. But Global Islamism is not concerned with those facts. It wants to 'liberate' all of Arabia from all foreign – non-Muslim – presence (though where this leaves Arab Christians is another matter). The message is 'Get rid of Israel and remove the Americans from Saudi soil.' But again it is given to 'every Muslim'. In Sunni Islam, there is no hierarchy of clergy whereby such calls can only be issued by some designated imam. So no one can question the bona fides of Bin Laden and his companions in issuing such a call to jihad.

After 9/11, Osma Bin Laden developed this theme further and extended the historical background to the First World War. Thus in October 2001 he said:

> What America is tasting today is but a fraction of what we have tasted for decades. For over eighty years our *umma* has endured this humiliation and contempt. ... So when God Almighty granted

success to one of the vanguard groups of Islam, He opened the way
for them to destroy America utterly. (2001: 104)

This eighty-year theme was elaborated in another letter to Al-
Jazeera in November 2001:

> Since World War One, which ended over 83 years ago, the entire
> Islamic world has fallen under the Crusader banners, under the
> British, French and Italian governments. They divided up the whole
> world between them, and Palestine fell into the hands of the British.
> From that day to this, more than 83 years later, our brothers and
> sons have been tortured in Palestine. Hundreds of thousands of
> them have been killed, hundreds of thousands detained. Then look
> at recent events, for example in Chechnya. This Muslim nation
> has been attacked by the Russian predator, which believes in the
> Orthodox Christian creed. The Russians have exterminated an
> entire people and forced them into mountains, where they have been
> devoured by disease and freezing winter, and yet no one has done
> anything about it. Then there is the genocidal war in Bosnia that
> took place in front of the whole world's eyes and ears. For several
> years, even in the heart of Europe, our brothers were murdered, our
> women raped, and our children slaughtered in the safe havens of
> the United Nations, and with its knowledge and cooperation. (2001:
> 135–6)

The strategy here is to link the present tragedies that Muslims in
different parts of the world face, for each of which there may be a
specific, contingent explanation in the Western mind (and even as
a matter of fact), with the central event of the fall of the Ottoman
Empire and its break-up by the victorious powers of Britain and
France. This linking is what makes Global Islamism a powerful
ideology. Bin Laden does not acknowledge that soon after the
massacre of Bosnian Muslims in Srebrenica, Western troops did
finally stop the ethnic cleansing and liberate Bosnian Muslims just

as he gives no credit to the coalition in Desert Storm for rescuing Kuwait. There is no connection, for example, between what happened in Chechnya and the Ottoman Empire, unless one goes back to the nineteenth century when the tsar was in an endemic war with the Sultan. Bin Laden does not go that far back since he wishes to maintain the link with the West rather than be detracted by the battles between the Romanov and the Ottoman empires.

The long passage quoted above is followed by a strong denunciation of the UN. Here again, Bin Laden focuses sharply on sensitive issues. Thus, he first denounces Muslim leaders for collaborating with the UN:

> Those who maintain that they are the leaders of the Arabs and are still part of the United Nations are contravening what was revealed to Muhammad. Those who refer to international legitimacy have contravened the legitimacy of the Qur'an and the teachings of the Prophet. (136)

Now, it is not at all clear how support for the UN contravenes 'the legitimacy of the Qur'an, or what was revealed to Muhammad'. The UN is held responsible for the setting up of the State of Israel, of course. But the implicit message is that the only legitimate empire which does not contravene the Qur'an is an Islamic empire, presumably covering the whole world. Bin Laden invokes those vague memories of the days when Islam was a universal imperial power. (Even at its height in the eighth to the fourteenth centuries, there were rival empires and kingdoms facing Islam, but Osama Bin Laden finds it convenient to see the Islamic empire as universal.) Everything that happened after that is illegitimate. The rights of a Muslim country override all other rights. Thus he dislikes the independence of East Timor. In the same statement, in the course of denouncing the UN, he says:

> Look at the position of the West and the United Nations with regard to events in Indonesia. They moved to partition the most populous nation in the Islamic world. The criminal Kofi Annan publicly put pressure on the Indonesian government, telling it that it had 24 hours to partition and separate East Timor from Indonesia, otherwise he would have to introduce military forces to do it. The Crusader armies of Australia were on the shores of Indonesia and they did in fact intervene and separate East Timor, which is part of the Islamic world. (137)

The idea clearly is that any territory that an 'Islamic' country has taken over, whether legitimately or not, should not be taken away from it. To speak of the 'partitioning of Indonesia' in the case of East Timor is bizarre. The invasion of East Timor by Indonesia only prolonged its liberation from foreign rule; only the nationality of the foreign ruler changed. Nevertheless, Bin Laden's words will appeal to many Muslims, especially in Indonesia, who are sensitive to centuries of hurt from the Dutch rulers. For Bin Laden it helps that almost every quarrel can be referred back to the First World War. Recalling the Hashemite dynasty's doings, Bin Laden said in a 2004 tape-recording which was played on Al-Jazeera:

> As for foreign policy, the ruling families have responded to America's wishes, leading the way in treachery. King Hussein of Jordan, for example, continued the policy of betrayal started against Palestine by his grandfather Abdallah bin al-Sharif Hussein, as well as his father. (2004: 253)

This is the Hussein whose father Hussein ibn Ali was the Sharif of Mecca and who collaborated with the British to fight the Ottoman Sultan. He had of course hoped for a lot of territory in an independent Arabia but he got Transjordan. He took the title of Caliph from the Ottoman Sultan but was defeated by the Saud family, who took the title of Sharif of Mecca.

What Does Global Islamism Want?

Surrender from Saudi Arabia

Osama Bin Laden's main quarrel in Arabia is of course with the Saud family. He offers them the following programmatic option:

> You therefore now have a choice between two paths.
>
> One: to restore to the people trusteeship in a peaceful way and to let the people of the country choose a Muslim ruler who will rule according to God's book, and the *hadith* of his Prophet.
>
> Two: to refuse to give people their rights back, to continue oppressing them and depriving them of their rights, to exploit certain people by paying them money out of the nation's public funds so that they can beat and kill their brothers and cousins who have rejected your authority. But you should know that things have gone far enough already, and that when people rise up to demand their rights no security apparatus can stop them. Don't forget what happened to the Shah of Iran despite the reputation, strength, and experience of his security apparatus, or what happened to Ceauşescu in Romania and the terrible fate that he and his family met for what he did to his people. So clearly you would be better off if you restore to the people their rights. (2004: 273)

The example of the Iranian Revolution and of Ayatollah Khomeini has obviously impressed Bin Laden. He does not of course explicitly refer to the Ayatollah as he belongs to the dissident Shi'a sect. But the similarity in the power of the Shah, his high standing as an ally of the West, his powerful secret service Savak as well as the suddenness of his collapse will all be known and remembered by Muslims. The Shah had just invented for himself a 2500 year history of his dynasty (which in reality had a history of less than fifty years) and crowned himself in a glamorous ceremony to which many Western leaders and media were lured. He had also bought modern arms from the West. But Khomeini had been a thorn in his side and fought him over twenty years, first from Najaf and then from Paris. He also circulated tape recordings of his sermons, which were popular in the Tehran bazaars. It was the steady drip drip of the Ayatollah's campaign and the failure of the Shah's White Revolution that together scuttled him.[32] Bin Laden's career has been somewhat more well known than the Ayatollah's and he has taken on more than just the Saudi family. Yet his hopes arise from that example. When he invites the Saudis to 'choose a Muslim ruler who will rule according to God's book', he perhaps means himself.

Destruction of the American Superpower

Bin Laden has also been sustained by the experience of witnessing the defeat of the Soviet Union's army in Afghanistan. In his first declaration of jihad in 1996, from which I have already quoted, he refers in passing to

> The peaks of the Hindu Kush, the very same peaks upon which were smashed, by the grace of God, the largest infidel military force in the world. (1996: 26–7)

Of course he does not mention the American and Pakistani contribution to the effort. But the Soviet incursion into Afghanistan was Bin Laden's call to dedicate himself to fighting for the Muslim cause.

> Praise be to God, Lord of the Worlds, that He made it possible for us to aid the *mujahidin* in Afghanistan without any declaration of

jihad [but instead through] the news that was broadcast by radio stations that the Soviet Union invaded a Muslim country. This was a sufficient provocation for me to start to aid our brothers in Afghanistan. (1997: 48)

The Soviet Union had been invited by the then Communist government of Afghanistan rather than having invaded the country. But this is a small detail for Bin Laden. It is also interesting that he had not reacted when Afghanistan experienced a Communist takeover but only when the Soviet Union went to the aid of its Communist ally. Bin Laden shows an understanding of the realpolitik of the Cold War when he speaks of the reason the Soviet Union came to the Afghan government's aid.

One look at a map would tell you that Afghanistan was not so much a target in itself, but was rather a passage for the Soviet forces, after they had achieved large gains in the world at that time. For the Russians thought that they could strike a decisive blow to the West by occupying the Straits of Hormuz and all the Gulf states, thereby taking possession of the biggest petroleum reserves in the world. (48)

This is another version of Kipling's 'Great Game', but there is also the implication that, if he were to become the ruler of Saudi Arabia, as he invites the Saudi royal family to abdicate in his favour, he would control all that petroleum. No wonder the Americans have announced a $25 million prize for his capture. Yet the main point is not autobiographical, as he added:

So our experience in this jihad was great, by the grace of God, praise and glory be to Him, and what we benefited from most was that the myth of the superpower was destroyed not only in my mind but also in the minds of all Muslims. Slumber and fatigue vanished and so did the terror which the US would use in its media by attributing to itself superpower status or which the Soviet Union used by labelling itself as a superpower. (1998: 82)

So the connection between the proven fragility of one superpower and the expected fragility of the other one is clear in Bin Laden's mind. He gives Somalia as an example,

We believe that America is much weaker than Russia, and we have learned from our brothers who fought in the jihad in Somalia of the incredible weakness and cowardice of the American soldier. Not even eighty of them had been killed and they fled in total darkness in the middle of the night, unable to see a thing. (82)

By 2001, after 9/11, he had convinced himself that America could be defeated even more easily than the Soviet Union.

The Soviet Empire has become – with God's grace – a figment of the imagination. Today, there is no more Soviet Empire; it split into smaller states and only Russia is left. So the One God, who sustained us with one of His helping Hands and stabilized us to defeat the Soviet Empire, is capable of sustaining us again and of allowing us to defeat America on the same land, and with the same sayings. So we believe that the defeat of America is something achievable – with the permission of God – and it is easier for us – with the permission of God – than the defeat of the Soviet Empire previously. (2001: 109)

Bin Laden's confidence is compounded of his experience with the Soviet Union and the American scuttle from Somalia, to which he returns in the further answer to the question that he answered in the quotation above. Yet there he was in the middle of the second week of war on Afghanistan (which the Taliban promptly lost within a week) and sanguine about defeating America. But he also boasts about the stock market collapse in the wake of 9/11. The loss was 16 per cent of the value of the stocks quoted on Wall

Street; he calculates that this, as a fraction of the $4 trillion worth of securities quoted on Wall Street, represents $640 billion. He adds to this the cost of disruption of work by citing the American payroll at $20 billion a day; a week of disruption he says amounts to $140 billion. Soon he reaches $1 trillion as the damage he has done 'due to the successful and blessed attacks'.

Of course, this is fanciful arithmetic. The stock market can come down one day and recover the next so what is lost is what Marx called 'fictitious capital'. Nor did all of America stop work for a week, even if the daily income is $20 billion. But he has clearly taken heart from the damage the attack caused. He also notes with some mockery that America has censored the broadcasting of his words in the wake of the 9/11 attack. He says:

> It is that this Western civilization, which is backed by America, has lost its values and appeal. The immense materialistic towers, which preach Freedom, Human Rights, and Equality, were destroyed. These values were revealed as a total mockery, as was made clear when the US government interfered and banned the media outlets from airing our words (which don't exceed a few minutes) because they felt that the truth started to appear to the American people, and that we aren't really terrorists in the way they want to define the term, but because we are being violated in Palestine, in Iraq, in Lebanon, in Sudan, in Somalia, in Kashmir, in the Philippines, and throughout the world, and that this is a reaction from the young men of our *umma* against the violations of the British Government. (112–13)

The last sentence above hints at the Sykes–Picot Agreement of 1916. Thus, once again, the past and the present are connected, as are the various contemporary struggles that involve Muslims. He points out quite cynically the impact the 9/11 attack has had on the urgency of solving the Palestine question. The road map that

President Bush put forward and urged on Ariel Sharon, asserts Bin Laden, is thanks to the mayhem caused by the attack on the Twin Towers. It will be denied, and not without reason, that any such link existed, but his rhetoric is cogent.

> So the declarations of the leaders, both in the East and the West, stated that the causes and roots of terrorism have to be removed. When they were asked to identify these causes, they mentioned the Palestine issue. We are part of a rightful cause, but in the fear of America, these countries could not say that our cause is just – so they call us terrorists, and then ask us to fix the Palestine issue. In light of these recent attacks and what ensued from them, Bush and Blair quickly reacted and said now is the time to create an independent nation for Palestine. Amazing! And yet there was apparently no suitable time in the last 10 years to address the issue before the 9/11 attacks happened? They evidently won't wisen up without the language of beatings and killings. So, as they kill us, without a doubt we have to kill them, until we obtain a balance in terror. This is the first time, in recent years, that the balance of terror has evened out between the Muslims and the Americans. (114)

Thus, Bin Laden sees the battle as a global battle between his side, unilaterally representing the *umma*, and the Americans and their allies – much as the Marxists claimed to do for the workers of the world. It is of course a guerrilla war fought in many theatres around the world where Muslims are fighting their battles. But, with 9/11, he has also taken the battle to the US mainland itself. This is the boldest move in the global guerrilla war. Since when, of course, the war has been waged in Spain, Indonesia (but really against the Australian tourists in Bali), Sharm-el-Sheikh, London and elsewhere. Since Bush talked of a crusade, he inadvertently spoke the language that Bin Laden has been using. He has been talking of the crusader with Jewish or Christian epithets attached to the word. With Bush's speech on 16 September 2001, Bin Laden feels vindicated.

> So Bush has declared in his own words: 'Crusade attack'. The odd thing about this is that he has taken the words right out of our mouth [that this war is a crusade]. Some people also believe what is said about us, like the [Saudi] Minister's words, that we declare other Muslims to be unbelievers – we seek God's refuge from this. But when Bush speaks, people make apologies for him and they say that he didn't mean to say that this war is a crusade, even though he himself said that it was! ... Bush's image today is of him being in the front of the line, yelling and carrying his big cross. And I swear by God Almighty, that whoever walks behind Bush or his plan has rejected the teachings of Muhammad, and this ruling is one of the clearest rulings in the Book of God and the *hadith* of his Prophet; and ... the proof for this is the Almighty's words while addressing the true believers: 'O you who believe! Take not the Jews and the Christians as allies, they are but allies to one another. And if any amongst you takes them as allies, then surely he is one of them.'
> (121–2)

The Qur'anic quotation takes us right back to the seventh century in Arabia where Muhammad had to fight the tribes which had been converted to Judaism or Christianity but which in his view had lapsed from the message of God. Many people when they hear something like this put it in the modern post-Holocaust context and immediately see an anti-Semitic angle to Bin Laden and indeed to Islam. But the way in which Islam sees itself is worth understanding. The idea is that God gave the world Islam at its very beginning. He sent Adam and Eve into exile from the Garden of Eden. He then sent many prophets, among them Moses and Abraham and Jesus. But people kept on not getting the true message and drifting off into apostasy or just darkness – *jahiliya*. So God finally sent Muhammad as his last messenger and chose him for a direct revelation of his word. So Islam is just the best version of Judaism and Christianity, and the latter should see the light and embrace their true religion as revealed by their God – the one and only God – to his chosen but the last Prophet. After Muhammad, there are no more prophets as there is no need. The Qur'an as revealed to Muhammad is God's final word. The Jewish and Christian Prophets are part of Islam's prophets, but only Muhammad is the Prophet, with a capital P.[33]

It is this background that allows Bin Laden to stake Muslim claim to Israel (not Palestine) itself. In his most explicit address to the Americans, posted on the Internet in October 2002, he makes his programme and his goals starkly explicit. The text repeats much of what we have already seen by way of the history of Muslims in the twentieth century. But then he faces up to two frequently asked questions:

1. Why are we fighting and opposing you?
2. What are we calling you to, and what do we want from you?

It is in the course of answering the first question that Bin Laden starts with the issue of Israel/Palestine. After asserting that 'The creation of Israel is a crime which must be erased', he makes the following astounding assertion:

It brings us both laughter and tears to see that you have not tired of repeating your fabricated lies that the Jews have a historical right to Palestine, as it was promised to them in the Torah. Anyone who disputes with them on this alleged fact is accused of anti-semitism. This is one of the most fallacious, widely-circulated fabrications in history. The people of Palestine are pure Arabs and original Semites. It is the Muslims who are the inheritors of Moses (peace be upon him) and the inheritors of the real Torah that has not been changed. Muslims believe in all of the Prophets, including Abraham, Moses, Jesus and Muhammad. If the followers of Moses have been promised a right to Palestine in the Torah, then the Muslims are the most worthy nation of this.

When the Muslims conquered Palestine and drove out the Romans, Palestine and Jerusalem returned to Islam, the religion of all the Prophets. Therefore, the call to a historical right to Palestine cannot be raised against the Islamic *umma* that believes in all the Prophets of God – and we make no distinction between them. (2002: 162)

Such a proposition will be regarded as far-fetched if not outrageous. But in one sense Bin Laden shrewdly exploits his *faux naïveté* about Islam being the only religion that envelops the two previous mono-theisms of the Middle East. Thus he seriously wants Americans to convert to Islam. In the answer to the second question above, he says: 'The first thing we are calling you to is Islam' (166).

Bin Laden calls Islam 'the seal of all the previous religions', by which he means Judaism and Christianity. He does not admit the existence of any other religion – Buddhism, Hinduism or Zoro-astrianism. He invites the Americans to accept 'complete submis-sion to His Laws; and the discarding of all the opinions, orders, theories, and religions which contradict the religion He sent down to His Prophet Muhammad' (166). But he is not that naive and does not pursue this matter further; the bulk of his answer is de-voted to a critique of the American way of life in all its aspects. The very first injunction gives a flavour of what is to follow:

We call you to be a people of manners, principles, honor, and purity; to reject the immoral acts of fornication, homosexuality, intoxicants, gambling, and usury. (166)

In short, give up Life, Liberty and the Pursuit of Happiness, many Americans might say. He does not approve of the fact that America is ruled by the Constitution and its own made laws rather than the Sharia. He hates usury, which is permitted in America. He denounces gambling, sexual exposure and the exploitation of sex, sale of drugs and alcohol. He accuses America of having exported HIV/AIDS to the world (quite falsely of course), of not signing up to the Kyoto Agreement (quite rightly), of preventing the spread of democracy abroad, of aiding Israel to flout UN resolutions, of seeking immunity from the International Criminal Court for Americans while pursuing foreign war criminals, of monitoring the human rights performance of other countries while allowing Guantánamo Bay to exist for the incarceration of prisoners without conviction.

The political set of demands however are starkly presented at the end of this statement. Among them are

- Stop supporting Israel, the Indians in Kashmir, the Russians against the Chechens and the Manila Government against the Muslim guerrillas.
- Get out of our lands, do not force us to send you back as cargo in coffins.
- End your support for our corrupt leaders or else expect us in New York and Washington.
- Deal with us on the basis of mutual interests and benefits, rather than the policies of subjugation, theft and occupation.

The entire message ends with a warning that if his demands are not heeded, Americans will lose the crusade Bush has launched.

If you Americans do not respond, then your fate will be that of the Soviets who fled from Afghanistan to deal with their military defeat, political breakup, ideological downfall, and economic bankruptcy. (172)

Evaluating the Global Islamist Ideology

Global Islamism is a complex construction with a simple theme. It is an account of the Muslim predicament during the last hundred or so years. What was once a great and universal empire has disappeared, and a people once proud and world-conquering is now adrift. They have no single spiritual or temporal authority for the first time in thirteen centuries. The response is to ask who is to blame for the current malaise. The poet Muhammad Iqbal engaged himself in a dialogue with Allah, but at the end blamed Muslims themselves for their plight. Global Islamism does not accept such an analysis. It puts the onus squarely on the West: on the Sykes–Picot Agreement of 1916 and the Balfour Declaration of 1917, which together partitioned the Middle East into various territories for which Britain and France acquired mandates. This complaint then jumps thirty years and blames the West and the UN for the creation of Israel, a nation which the Arabs have tried thrice to destroy but failed. The blame for Israel's continued survival then shifts to America, which has stood by Israel for the last thirty years at least. (In 1948 it was the USSR that came to Israel's aid; in 1956 the USA prevented Britain, France and Israel from invading Egypt.)

This basic story is then embellished by weaving together the many theatres of conflict where Muslims are involved – Kashmir, Chechnya, Bosnia, Afghanistan, the Philippines – and America is held responsible for the plight of Muslims. Inconsistencies and unilateral behaviour on America's part are added to the mixture to make a case that Global Islamism is justified in launching terrorist attacks against America and Americans. This historical argument is then clothed in messianic terms and the Qur'an is quoted and the

Prophet's name repeatedly invoked. The essence of the argument is still a political/historical one. Many have made the same argument of inconsistency against America on left-wing and/or secular grounds. At present in Latin America, leaders such as Fidel Castro of Cuba and Hugo Chávez of Venezuela are making a similar argument. In Bolivia and Chile, left-wing candidates came to power in early 2006 and will no doubt echo some of the same arguments.

What is peculiar about the Global Islamist story, its terrorism apart, is that it is an entirely self-serving and uncritical account of the Muslim predicament. It portrays the decline of Muslims as a unique event caused entirely by external forces. In this, it is similar to the rhetoric of many colonial nationalist movements which used to blame every ill on the imperial power, and exonerated themselves from all blame. It was only after independence that many of these nationalist movements learnt that government and development were not just a matter of getting rid of the foreign ruler but examining their own resources and shortcomings. Muslims of Arabia were, however, not subjects of a foreign master, but members of an imperial nation which ruled over many ethnic minorities. These minorities were treated as equally inferior and tolerated, but never perceived as equal to the Muslims. The non-Muslims had to pay a special tax for being non-Muslims – the *jaziya*. From such a privileged position, Muslims fell to a condition of equality with people of other religions, when the Ottoman Empire disintegrated.

The origin of Muslim misery is arguably due not to foreign machinations but entirely to the weakness of the Ottoman Empire, mainly because of its failure to adapt to modern trends of industrialization with the shift to a scientific and rational mode of thinking.[34] This weakness of the Ottoman Empire could not be solved by a return to the faith, but only by moving forward to receive the benefits of Enlightenment. Colonies of Asia further east, like India, Malaya and Indonesia, in this respect were harnessed to a modernisation programme much more effectively than the Ottoman Empire. This is why the Muslims of those countries have had a different trajectory than the Arabs of the Middle East. India, for example, felt the challenge of modernity by the middle of the nineteenth century at the latest, and both Hindu and Muslim communities had to respond. The Muslim community adopted, like the Hindu community, the twin paths of reform and revival, with Sir Syed Ahmad extolling the virtues of western education and the Deobandi movement offering a cautious mixture of revival with awareness of modern developments.[35] In 2006 the president of India is a Muslim who is also a leading scientist and a designer of India's missile programme. Muslims have prospered in Malaysia and Indonesia, though there is a lot further yet for their economies to go. The Ottoman Empire in a way sheltered Muslims from the full challenge of modernity. When it collapsed, the shock was total. Nevertheless, what happened to the Ottoman Empire was not unique.

The break-up of the Ottoman Empire was due to a defeat in the First World War but it was not the only empire to break up. The Habsburg Empire, which ruled over much of central, southern and eastern Europe, an inheritor of the Holy Roman Empire, of equal antiquity to the caliphate, also vanished. Its constituent regions became independent nations just like those of the Ottoman Empire. Many became satellites of the Soviet Union after the Second World War and are now members of the European Union or aspiring to join. The people of these nations have not had a trouble-free trajectory through the twentieth century yet they have not told themselves a story which blames America or Russia for all their ills.

Later still after the Second World War, the British, French, Belgian and Dutch empires broke up, with many countries becoming independent. While these post-imperial nations of Europe have developed at an uneven pace, they are not hankering for a return to some primeval state when they were great empires (though a few extreme right-wing fascists in these countries do), but again marching forward to adapt their economies and societies to new challenges. Their ex-colonies are marching ahead as well. China is a case in point: it suffered the humiliation of foreign interference in its affairs, but bounced back and is now a world power. India is a similar case though still a bit behind China. South Korea and Taiwan used to be colonies of Japan but have become highly developed countries. It is only the Global Islamists who choose to dwell on an 83-year-old story recalling every slight and every betrayal. There is no introspection as to whether the failure to develop could have anything to do with the people themselves and the nations which emerged from the Ottoman Empire or with the unreformed nature of the society, sunk in religiosity.

The majority of Muslims of the world live outside Arabia, outside the boundaries of the former Ottoman Empire. Many millions live in majority Muslim countries and enjoy democratic freedoms – Malaysia and Indonesia for example. Some 144 million Muslims – the second largest Muslim population in the world – live in India as a minority but within a democracy. Pakistan, the third largest Muslim country, has been a democracy half of its 59 years of independence, and may become a democracy again soon. The trick that Global Islamism performs is to include all Muslims in the plight of the Arab Muslims. For this reason local conflicts such as Kashmir are made part of the global story. But often this can be done only by reducing the conflict to a simple good and evil caricature. Take Kashmir for instance.

The Kashmir Problem

The problem of Kashmir is a complex one since it arises from the disputed basis of the Partition of India. Before 1947 when both India and Pakistan became independent, the British ruled over the undivided India. But they did not rule over the entire territory. British India so-called accounted for two-thirds of India's territory and six hundred 'princely states', with Indian kings occupying the remaining one-third. The kings were under the 'paramountcy' of the British viceroy, who represented the British emperor. The viceroy, doubled as governor general, was ruler of British India, appointed by Parliament. At the time of Partition, Lord Mountbatten was the viceroy–governor general.

In partitioning the then undivided India, separate criteria were used on the basis of which provinces of British India were apportioned between India and Pakistan as against the princely states. The former were allocated on the basis of religion and population, so that provinces with a Muslim majority went to Pakistan. Two large provinces, Punjab and Bengal, which had just a bare majority of Muslims over the rest, were divided with one half going to Pakistan (West Punjab and East Bengal) and the other half going to India (East Punjab and West Bengal). The rulers of the six hundred princely states, which had a third of the total population of pre-Partition India, were given a choice which country to join. Most of them signed up with their contiguous nation-state, India or Pakistan. Two princely states that were contiguous to India but sought independence, Hyderabad and Junagadh, were forced into India by 'police action'. They both had a Hindu majority population and a Muslim king.

The princely state of Jammu and Kashmir had a Muslim majority mainly in the Kashmir valley, while Hindus were largely in majority in Jammu. It was also situated at the border of both India and Pakistan. Thus contiguity did not yield a clear decision whether the king should join India or Pakistan. So the state's Hindu king delayed his accession decision, hoping to drive a hard bargain with one of the two powers. But in the meantime, irregular troops from Pakistan marched towards Srinagar, the capital, to remove him and absorb the state forcibly into Pakistan. He signed up with India hours before he was about to lose his capital. Thus there was a war between the two newly independent countries which were only a few months previously part of the same polity. The UN intervened and declared a ceasefire with a Line of Control separating the Kashmir valley. India agreed to holding a plebiscite among the people of Jammu and Kashmir to elicit their wishes as to whether they wanted to join India or Pakistan. This would have made Jammu and Kashmir an exception among all the princely states. As the years passed India reneged on that promise to hold a plebiscite on the grounds that various other conditions of the UN resolution were not complied with by Pakistan. But Jammu and Kashmir (at least the part retained in India) has enjoyed, like the rest of India, a democratic government.

The dispute has festered since 1948. The two countries have fought four wars over it, and more recently mujahideen groups from Pakistan, trained by al-Qaeda, have descended on Kashmir. India takes the view that Kashmir is an integral part of Indian territory, and that its future status is non-negotiable on any other basis except its continuation as a part of India. Pakistan takes the view that the Kashmir dispute is still unsettled, since the promised plebiscite of the people of Kashmir has never taken place. Within Indian Kashmir there have been elections since 1948, though any impartial observer would admit that Indian government has often behaved in a high-handed way towards Kashmiri leaders. Jammu and Kashmir had been promised a special status within the Constitution of India, but the state is now treated just like any other state. As happens elsewhere in India, chief ministers have been replaced by their rivals within the ruling party at the behest of Delhi. In particular, for many years India incarcerated Shaikh Abdullah, who was the undisputed leader of the National Conference Party of Jammu and Kashmir, the first chief minister (prime minister). His son Farooq inherited his popularity and became chief minister of Kashmir later in the 1980s.

Since 1989, Kashmir has been subject to infiltration by terrorist groups from across the border. These groups, under labels such as Lashkar-e-Toiba and Jaish-e-Mohammad, have received training in the Afghan camps run by al-Qaeda, and their declared aim is to integrate Kashmir back into the Islamic state which they hope Pakistan can become. India has deployed a massive military presence to combat these incursions. There is also a large Pakistani army on the Pakistan side of Kashmir across the Line of Control. There have been frequent attacks in the rest of India by some of the groups, in Delhi, Mumbai and (in January 2006) in Bangalore at an academic conference.

Today there is a democratically elected government in Kashmir but there are also groups which are in favour of other solutions, including joining Pakistan or the creation of an independent Kashmir. In Pakistani Kashmir, called Azad (Free) Kashmir, there have also been governments elected. In October 2005, Azad Kashmir suffered a severe earthquake, which also affected parts of Indian Kashmir. The suffering brought home to anyone who wished to see it the heavy price paid by the people of Kashmir due to a nationalist quarrel between India and Pakistan over their territory.

Kashmir is a bilateral dispute between India and Pakistan and not a problem created by America. Britain quit India sixty years ago, and is not being blamed by either country for the dispute. There has been a great deal of negotiation between the two sides and also between the various dissident groups in Kashmir with both governments. This problem, difficult as it is, is not insoluble. It is also not a problem of Muslims against non-Muslims, since millions of Muslims live in Kashmir as well as in both India and Pakistan. Indeed if one includes Bangladesh, which was part of Pakistan until it broke free in 1971, one-third of the world's Muslim population lives on the Indian subcontinent. Kashmir is a problem of competing nationalisms and not one of Muslims against the rest.

An eventual solution for Kashmir is elusive but the general principles on which a solution will be viable can be easily stated. Four wars have shown that Pakistan cannot snatch Kashmir from India by military force, and the same wars and the persistence of unrest and terrorism have proved that while India has possession of

Kashmir it will not enjoy a peaceful possession if it does not agree to rethink the status quo. Thus each side must be denied its preferred option. But each has its second-best option, which involves the other side not getting full control of Kashmir. This can be assured if we can have a merger of the two parts of Kashmir across the Line of Control, demilitarisation of both parts and the creation of an autonomous Kashmir belonging neither to India nor to Pakistan exclusively but whose military security is guaranteed by both, perhaps with the G8 or the UN Security Council Permanent Members. In disputes such as these, where rival nationalisms claim the same piece of land, there is no stable solution except to share the land, since neither can have an absolute claim while it does not command 100 per cent support of the people living on the land. How soon such a solution will be implemented is an open question. But, to repeat, it is not an issue of Muslims versus non-Muslims.

Conclusion

I have dwelt at some length on the Kashmir dispute because it is easy to string it into the single global story, as Bin Laden does; yet it does not belong there unless you blame every event of the twentieth century on imperialism. The problem in the Chechen republic arises from the peculiarity of the Russian Constitution, with its provisions for autonomy, and the crisis of post-USSR Russia. Russia's violation of human rights in Chechnya has been criticised by the West, but the doctrine of national sovereignty prevents further interference. Human rights were violated when Iraq invaded Kuwait, and the international community did come to the rescue of Kuwaiti Muslims, but Bin Laden takes that as aggression by Americans. So even among Muslims, he only cares for the rights of some, not all. He says nothing about the Iran–Iraq war, which lasted eight years and took a million lives, since he is only interested in faulting Western powers, not in protecting Muslim lives as such.

Global Islamism shares with many Western and other critiques a scathing view of America's inconsistencies and hypocrisies (as well of its many allies, especially the UK). It notes the asymmetric importance of Israel in America's foreign policy, as many have done. As I have mentioned above, Edward Said, Noam Chomsky, Gore Vidal, Mahmood Mamdani and many other critics would be in agreement with much of the political criticism of America. They would, however not share the moralistic vision of Bin Laden, which is against homosexuality and disapproves of drink and drugs, gambling and usury. The essence of freedom is the right to choose a lifestyle which need not conform to that of the majority, or indeed of anybody else, as long as it does not harm others.

Where Global Islamism parts company with many critics is in its resort to the threat of perpetual violence, of guerrilla warfare. Many may also object that if Bin Laden were to get his victory life would be intolerable for millions of non-Muslims, since his notion of justice requires all to be Muslims or suffer endless humiliation, if not death. Although he is critical of America's double standards on human rights, his own views, as seen from his remarks on Iraq's invasion of Kuwait and East Timor, are that Muslim countries have a right to invade other countries and subjugate them. Since, in his view, there is no possibility of debate or doubt over what the Qur'an lays down (although in real life there are many quarrels about interpretations and his is only one of them), his vision of the world will be the exact opposite of what any tolerant, liberal person would like.

Yet we have to take the ideology of Global Islamism seriously if only to know how to combat it. It is to this task that I turn in the next chapter.

FIVE

Combating Global Islamism

Global Islamism poses the most serious military challenge to the world and not just the West. Its acts of global guerrilla warfare have taken lives of Muslims and non-Muslims around the world – Bali, Madrid, London, Delhi, New York, Sharm-el-Sheikh, Amman. Its challenge is that it will use violence against civilians and soldiers alike until the West quits Arabia and ultimately adopts Islam. While it has a cogent critique of many inconsistencies in Western foreign policies, in itself it is an illiberal and intolerant doctrine, albeit clothed in the universalist language of Islam. To combat it one has to separate it from Islam and its practices. What is at dispute is no theological or doctrinal question, no question of interpretation of the Qur'an or the Hadith.

Many well-meaning people have asked for an understanding of Islam, a dialogue between the many faiths, an ecumenical coming together. While all these things are desirable on their own, they are beside the point when it comes to combating Global Islamism. It is not interested either in a dialogue with other faiths, or in an ecumenical embrace. As Bin Laden's remarks on the Muslim claim to the promise in the Torah make clear, if Global Islamism were to triumph, there would be only one religion for all if they want to stay alive. Its message is of a monopoly of monotheism, with violent consequences if you disagree.

It is as a political ideology that Global Islamism still appeals to many Muslims around the world. It is for this reason that it is necessary to take it seriously, since it is able to recruit across the world, either directly to its banner or by a loose franchising, inspiring others to follow its example. It appeals to a deep hurt in the Muslim psyche, and it is this hurt which we all need to understand. But we also need to mount a critique of the ideology since its presumptions are false in many ways, and its recipe for assuaging the hurt of the Muslims is counterproductive. It is not by terror but by self-emancipation and economic advancement in material and human development that the hurt of the Muslim psyche will be soothed.

Of course, even as we speak of the hurt to the Muslim psyche, we must not exaggerate the appeal of Global Islamism. By its terrorist acts, Global Islamism has drawn all the attention to itself so that many people almost think it is the only form of Islam around the world. In responding to it, politicians have adopted an uncritical textualist approach – reading the Qur'an in an uncritical fashion. But this is to grasp the problem on the terms of Global Islamism itself. The need is to put it instead in a perspective of the wider Muslim society. Global Islamism is not the whole of Islam; it is at best a small, very noisy and destructive ideology feeding off Islam. Millions of Muslims carry on their daily lives with the usual problems that we all face – jobs, money to spend, health and education, happiness in social relations and the joy of seeing children growing up healthy.

Muslims like any other community are divided by class, by ethnicity and by nationality. There are antagonisms within the community. The age-old civil war of Islam between Shi'a and Sunni, which erupted within years of the death of Muhammad, is one division which tears Muslims apart even to this day, as we witness in Iraq. There are other minor sects as well, like the Ahmadiyas who are the outcasts in many Muslim countries. The Muslim diaspora now spans the globe, and, in many countries, Muslims are parliamentarians, bankers, industrialists, scientists. They suffer being caricatured and sometimes racially abused, especially after 9/11. They encounter misunderstanding of their faith and culture. But, in this, they are much like other immigrant communities around the world. How many of us, after all, understand the religion of the Chinese population among us?

There is a great knowledge deficit in the West so far as the history of Islam is concerned. It is not a recent thing. The great philosophers and historians have a blind spot when it comes to Islam. Western historiography, even in the hands of universalistic philosophers like Hegel and Marx, has a hole where Islamic history is concerned. (But also, one must add, where Chinese, Japanese and to some extent Indian history is concerned.) Adam Smith and Karl Marx take their history as going from Ancient Greece and Rome to the Renaissance via the Dark Ages. The Dark Ages were not dark at all; for Muslims they were the glorious period of Islamic conquest of Europe and Asia. The transmission of Classical philosophy and science, as well as Indian mathematics, to the West was effected by Muslim scholars. The European Renaissance itself is unthinkable without Muslim input as the transmitter of Ancient Europe to itself. But we find nothing of this in the ambitious stadial theory of history of Adam Smith or the historical materialism of Karl Marx and Friedrich Engels. The fact that Spain was under Muslim rule for seven centuries, and that this itself was culturally fruitful to European science and technology, has not been acknowledged. The situation here is similar to the neglect until very recently in American history writing of the contributions of black and Native Americans. Now the Americans are trying their best to correct this lacuna, thanks to the Civil Rights Movement, which changed awareness of the neglected aspects of their nation's history.

We need a major attempt to integrate the history of Islamic culture and history into a balanced story of Western history, and indeed world history (and the same applies to Chinese and Indian history). This must not be confused with the current plethora of books about Islam and understanding Muslims. These books, in my view, err on the side of overemphasising the role of religion in Muslim culture. In many ways, it is the reversal of the modernist reforming trends, and the resurgence of textualist tendencies such as the Wahhabi school which have distanced Muslims from the sceptical rationalist tone of much modern life in the West. Religion is enjoying something of a revival in Western societies no doubt. But many who have become religious have taken to private and individualist paths to God rather than via the Church or some orthodoxy. Fundamentalist Christians and Jews remain exotic and slightly bizarre minorities at home. This is why the emphasis on religion in the Western Muslim diaspora strikes an odd note for many people. While we all must understand it, we also have to be critical of such religiosity, as one would of such tendencies in any other religious minority. I speak as an atheist, of course, but I believe that understanding Muslims solely through the prism of their religion, or privileging their preachers to speak on behalf of their community is unhelpful for non-Muslims but even more so for Muslims.

We must also re-examine the history of Western imperialism and indeed of the modern era – not in a spirit of self-flagellation or self-congratulation. Western imperialism, like everything else, was a complex dialectical movement in world history. It was an agent of change since it carried modernity in the shape of capitalism and bureaucratic rationality across the world. It was at same time an exploitative, cruel and racist episode.[36] Yet pre-imperialist periods in the history of Asia or Africa are free of neither exploitation, cruelty nor racism. Slavery did not originate in the transatlantic human trade to America; nor did aggression and arbitrary violence begin in 1492. Empires have been with us for a long time in human history; only now is it possible to contemplate their final end. That is thanks to modernity.

The hypocrisies of imperialism in the modern era are shocking not because they are unprecedented; far from it. They are shocking because Enlightenment and modernity make us expect better behaviour from human beings towards each other. At the heart of modernity is a cherished value, an aspiration towards an equality of status among all human beings, equal rights. This is why the American Declaration of Independence is a brilliant document; we can admire it and also criticise it for not matching its rhetoric of 'all men are created equal' with regard to the status of women, black slaves and Native Americans. We do not criticise papal encyclicals or chapters of the holy books on such grounds since we do not expect rationality or egalitarianism from them. Today we read egalitarianism into the holy books of religion, but they were used as ideological supports in the long history of hierarchical and unequal societies that existed since time immemorial. It is only in the last 250 years that we have begun to believe that an equality of status of all human beings is not just an aspiration but an achievable possibility. It is only this modernity that allows us to read an egalitarian message in our religious texts. It is only modernity that compels us to look on all regions of the world as equally deserving of respect for their history and cultures.

So we must look at the division of the territories of Arabia as we would at Africa and Asia. What is troublesome about the division of the territory of a defeated power among the victorious ones is not that it did not always happen. After all, that is how all empires are built up, and the Ottoman Empire or previous Islamic empires were no exceptions. The initial expansion of Islam was among the regions of the Byzantine Empire in the West and the Sassanian one in the East. The problem is that by the advent of the twentieth century, one expected better behaviour from the victors. Indeed the British and the French kept the Sykes–Picot Agreement secret precisely because it went against their public rhetoric. They had promised one thing to the Sharif of Mecca, and intended to deceive him. He may have been a traitor to his own Sultan, but even so the British and the French should have behaved better.

It is this distance between the rhetoric of equality or democracy or human rights and the practice that falls quite short which upsets not only the victims of such hypocrisy but the citizens in whose name governments conduct their affairs. Even today, foreign affairs are conducted in a less transparent fashion than domestic ones.

In international relations, there is a weak and ineffective rule of law and a more prevalent rule of power. Realpolitik is admitted as legitimate, and unequal power relations are reinforced quite ruthlessly. The United Nations itself embodies the inequalities of power in its structure by putting the Security Council and its five Permanent Members in a privileged position whereby their veto can prevent many decisions from being implemented. No wonder many Arab Muslim nations feel aggrieved that Israel is protected by the American veto. Of course if they had not tried to 'drive Israel into the sea' in the first place, three times in the first 25 years of its existence, Middle Eastern politics could have been different.

Israel–Palestine: One State or Two?

The single issue that fuels the Global Islamist creed, as it does many other terrorist groups in the Middle East, is the Israel–Palestine issue. It is beyond the scope of this book to settle the score on what is a very complex question with deep historical and religious roots. Yet an attempt must be made to understand the origins of the present predicament.

The idea of a nation is of recent origin; it has been with us from the eighteenth century onwards. The Dutch battle for liberation from the Spanish Empire was perhaps the first 'national' struggle. The American and the French revolutions in their own separate ways laid the solid foundations of nationalism. It took root at first in Europe in the nineteenth century during the Napoleonic wars and later in Asia, Africa and Latin America. The basis on which a 'people' becomes, or comes to define itself as, a 'nation' is in itself a topic that is subject to much debate among scholars.[37] Religion, language, a shared history, a defined territory – all these aspects have been cited as elements defining a nation, but against each there can be cited counter-examples which prove their inadequacy as sufficient to define a nation. But nations have to become states, the so-called nation-states for national aspirations to be fulfilled. Until the twentieth century, there were few independent nations which were nation-states.

It was after the First World War, as empires dissolved, that there was a veritable explosion in the formation of nation-states. Nations began to be formed as part of the anti-colonial struggle against empires, and often conflicting nations fought for recognition in the same territory. Thus, as already outlined in the previous chapter, the British left the Indian subcontinent with two nation-states, India and Pakistan, ostensibly on the ground of religion, the argument made by Jinnah and the Muslim League being that there were two nations within British-ruled India, one Hindu and the other Muslim. Yet after the Partition, both India and Pakistan contained large populations of Muslims. Today India has 144 million Muslims (14 per cent of its population); Pakistan has 140 million (97 per cent); while Bangladesh, which was part of Pakistan until 1971, has 115 million (88 per cent). In a sense, what was partitioned in 1947 was not the territory of the Indian subcontinent but the Muslim people inhabiting that territory. They were split into two, and later still into three, nation-states.

The three countries of the Indian subcontinent represent a wide range of national formations. Thus Bangladesh is a Muslim-majority state with a single language – Bengali – and a compact territory, which used to be East Bengal in pre-1947 India. In contrast to the one religion/one language/one territory Bangladesh, Pakistan has a majority religion, Islam, several languages and a territory which is compact but contains a disputed part of Kashmir. The split between Pakistan and Bangladesh showed that religion by itself was not a sufficient basis for nationhood. The language differences between the two parts of Pakistan, as well as the neglect of the East Pakistanis by the dominant West Pakistanis caused the rupture. India is a multi-religion, multi-language country with territory on the subcontinent including the disputed part of Kashmir but also the remote islands of Andaman and Nicobar. It has stayed a nation despite many differences, which have sometimes boiled over into conflict, as with the Sikh demand for Khalistan, a separate Sikh nation. But democracy has enabled India to retain its national unity.[38] Thus nations become nation-states on a variety of grounds.

The establishment of the State of Israel as a result of a UN resolution was one of the early achievements of the post-1945 settlement. The decision had widespread support, not least from all five Security Council Permanent Members. The resolution was passed on 29 November 1947. Fifty years previous to that, the first Zionist Congress was held in Basle, Switzerland. The Jews had been exiled from their ancient Biblical land for two millennia and had existed as minorities – often persecuted and reviled minorities – in many countries of Europe and indeed all over the world. The Jews were a nation without a territory. During the late nineteenth century, there began a movement to encourage the migration of Jews from Russia to Palestine, which was then a part of the Ottoman Empire. This was 'practical Zionism'. In 1896, Theodore Herzl wrote his book *Der Judenstaat*, the first articulate theoretical argument for a Jewish homeland. It was following Herzl's book that Zionism was launched as a political programme. The Basel Programme stated: 'The aim of Zionism is to create for the Jewish people a home in Palestine secured by public law.'[39] Herzl recorded in his diary 'At Basel, I founded the Jewish State. If I said this out loud today, I would be answered by universal laughter. Perhaps in five years, and certainly in fifty, everyone will know it' (3).

Yet Palestine was already populated by Arabs, most of them Muslims. Arab nationalism was not yet formed, as the Ottoman Empire was a Muslim kingdom to the head of which, the caliph, devout Muslims owed their loyalty. Thus the idea of a Palestinian nation or even an Arab (super)nation was non-existent at this time. (Of course once a national movement is articulated, it often discovers roots in much earlier times than previously realised. Every nation claims to be timeless.) There was a steady influx of Jewish settlers, mainly from Europe, into Palestine over the next fifty years. In 1917, of course, the Balfour Declaration had committed the British government to work towards a Jewish homeland. This was classic imperial behaviour but not unusual for that time, as almost all nations formed during the twentieth century were outcomes of imperial creation or imperial withdrawal. But from here onwards, Israel came to be seen as a creature of the West. As Avi Shlaim says,

> The unstated assumption of Herzl and his successors was that the Zionist movement would achieve its goal not through an understanding with the local Palestinians but through an alliance with the dominant great power of the day. ... The dominant great power in the Middle East changed several times in the course of the twentieth century; first it was the Ottoman Empire, after World War I it was Great Britain, and after World War II it was the United States. (5)

From the outset, the Zionist movement had to face the knotty problem; if the home of Jews was going to be Palestine (initially other 'empty' regions, like Argentina, were also proposed), how were a minority of Jews going to convince the already settled Arabs that they should let them settle as a nation with sovereign rights? They could have proposed assimilating with the Arabs and slowly expanding somewhat, as the refugees from Iran did in India and became the Parsee community. But from the beginning the Zionist movement saw itself as somehow superior to, more 'civilised' than, their future hosts. Although persecuted in the West, the Jews who joined the Zionist movement saw themselves as Europeans and hence imbibed all the arrogance of the European *'mission civilisa-trice'*. Thus Jabotinsky, who was a revisionist Zionist, said that Zionsim was 'not a return of the Jews to their spiritual homeland but an offshoot or implant of Western civilization in the East'. It was Jabotinsky who also proposed the doctrine of the 'Iron Wall' between the Jews settling in Palestine and the local Arabs. He wrote:

> We must either suspend our settlement efforts or continue them without paying attention to the mood of the natives. Settlement can thus develop under the protection of a force that is not dependent on the local population, behind an iron wall which they will be powerless to break down. (13)

The use of the word 'natives' is telling of the imperialist attitude adopted by these persecuted people. It is as if all Jews lived in Europe or America and were not scattered all over the world. Of course Jews lived in the East as well as the West, as the Israeli state found out when the Ashkenazim and the Sephardic Jews had to learn to live together.

A Palestinian national movement did crystallise in the interwar period, mainly as a reaction to the influx of Jewish settlers and the promise of the Balfour Declaration.

Britain had begun to have second thoughts about the Declaration already by 1922 when Winston Churchill as Secretary for the Colonies declared a policy which sought to restrict Jewish migration to Palestine and promised proportional representation for the two communities in any eventual government. Early Zionism was a part of a broad socialist movement in Europe, but during the interwar period it became more nationalist and hostile to any accommodation with the Arab population. Later still in Israel, there persisted the left/right split between the Labour Party and Likud, or more religious parties, with two very different visions of Israel as coexisting with the Palestinians or as dominating them from behind an 'Iron Wall'.

Arab unrest in the late 1930s led the British government, which had the Palestine Mandate, to propose a partition of Palestine into a small Jewish state of 5000 square kilometres and a large Arab state with a British enclave, including Jerusalem. Within two years Britain withdrew the partition plan and proposed an Arab state in which Jews would live in a minority. But then the Second World War broke out.

> A much stronger kind of Zionism was forged in the course of World War II, and the commitment to Jewish statehood became deeper and more desperate in the shadow of the Holocaust. On the one hand, the Holocaust confirmed the conviction of the Zionists that they had justice on their side in the struggle for Palestine; on the other, it converted international public opinion to the idea of an independent Jewish state. (24)

As mentioned above, the Irgun was formed as a militant group to attack the British presence in Palestine. An extreme offshoot of the Irgun, the Stern Gang was even more uncompromising against the British and even sought the support of the Axis Powers in its cause. Faced with terrorist unrest, the British referred the Palestine problem to the UN in February 1947. Nine months later, the UN passed its Resolution 181. There was to be a Jewish state and an Arab state, linked in an economic union, plus an international regime for Jerusalem. The Arab state was split into two territories in the middle of which was the Jewish state.

Neither side was happy with the proposal. The Stern Gang and Irgun wanted all of Palestine, especially Jerusalem, as part of the Jewish state. This is, according to many Jewish religious parties, the Biblical promise. The Palestinians denounced the proposal as 'absurd, impracticable and unjust'. The war that broke out upon the formation of Israel on 14 May 1948 resulted, as did the two subsequent wars, in a defeat for the Arab armies and a victory for Israel. The armistice signed at the end of the 1948–49 war meant that Israel had expanded its territory from around half of Palestine to around 75 per cent, and what should have been Palestine was absorbed by King Abdullah of Jordan into his kingdom. He changed the name of his kingdom from Transjordan to Jordan, and the newly grabbed part was called West Jordan or the West Bank, as it subsequently came to be known. This was in the words of Avi Shlaim 'the official demise of Arab Palestine'. It is ironic that in the very first moment of the creation of Israel and Palestine together, by means of a UN resolution, there followed a war between the Arab kingdoms and Israel with the consequence of an Arab king annexing a large chunk of Palestine, letting Israel claim the rest.

Thus was created the problem of Palestinian refugees, who fled to Egypt, Jordan, Syria and Lebanon. The Arab nations were as cynical in manipulating the refugees for their propaganda as they were indifferent to the plight of their fellow Arabs. Israel blamed the creation of the refugees on the attack by the Arab kingdoms in the first place. There was the usual UN resolution asking the refugees to be given a right to choose to return or be paid compensation for the loss of their homes, and as usual it was ignored.

Along the way, Israel has occupied illegally large portions of Palestinian territory, and Palestinians are dependent on Israeli goodwill to be able to work in Israel – on which their livelihood depends. Instead of an economic union, as was envisaged by UN Resolution 181, there is an asymmetry in the economic cooperation between Israel and the Palestinian territory. From its idealistic beginning on the left of the European political spectrum, Zionism has swung to a revisionist, 'Iron Wall' mentality of no compromise and constant military readiness to attack. Of course the Arab countries have obliged by playing the role Israeli leaders have imagined for them and twice again, in 1967 and 1973, invaded Israel. Israel in an aggressive defence posture attacked Lebanon in 1982. The international community has intervened again and again to procure ceasefire, if not peace, in the region. History repeated itself again in the month-long war of July–August 2006. The early sympathy for Israel is wearing thin as foreigners begin to see the Arab side of the argument better.

Despite promises given in various forums, including in the Oslo Accords, illegal settlements continued to be encouraged by Israeli governments in breach of international law. Had the initial hostility been absent then a two-state solution with an economic union would have made a lot of sense. After all, this is the path that France and Germany chose after fighting each other for nearly a century and today the European Union is a thriving prospect. Indeed, some idealists have hankered for a single multi-ethnic, multi-religious state where Arabs and Jews could live in peace together. In the example I gave above of the Indian subcontinent, one can have two countries with a single religion, single language and single territory like Bangladesh, or a multi-religious, multi-lingual territory like India. Lebanon has tried to create a multi-ethnic democracy against great hostility from Israel as well as from Syria. A single state where Jews and Palestinians can live on a basis of tolerance and equality would be an ideal solution since neither side can or should have an exclusive claim to the land. But perhaps that is now a distant dream. It would involve forgetting too much history and indeed setting aside many outside forces, which urge each of the two sides not to compromise. There is no doubt, however, that while Israelis have prospered, thanks to US aid but also to their effort and entrepreneurship, the Palestinians have suffered much economic hardship. Despite the illegality of Arab wars against Israel, the latter's occupation of Palestinian territory is also illegal. Israel blames the attacks by Palestinian groups on its population and property for its own tough stance.

In the latest conflict (July–August 2006) Israel fought Hezbollah in the north and Hamas in Gaza. Israel had withdrawn from Gaza, and Sharon had promised the same for the West Bank. Now under his successor Ehud Olmert, those steps will be reversed. This is yet another detour in the 60-year saga of Israel–Palestine relations, where each two steps forward are followed by a step and half backward.

A two-state solution remains not so much the best solution as the only viable one. Religion and nationalism are divisive, not uniting forces. In the Israel–Palestine case, each side has a combination of religion and nationalism as its rationale. It is a case of one piece of land with two strong claims on it, neither conceding the rights of the other nor willing to live together on a sharing basis. History is not much help here as the land has passed from one people to another over the last four thousand years. Also what happened to each people in their exile or their servile status adds complications. The complexities are baffling as they encompass not just the recent – twentieth-century – history of the region, but the entire four millennia of the region's history, as well as the modern history of Europe for the last several centuries, involved here. The demise of the European empires, the decline of Britain and the rise of the USA, the explosion of oil prices twice during the 1970s, and the death of the USSR, form the global context. No wonder the Israel–Palestine problem is such an emotionally charged one to debate, let alone settle.

Even so, Bin Laden's cynical statement that only 9/11 hastened the search for a solution of the Palestine problem should not go unchallenged. The history of the last thirty years, if not the last fifty, has witnessed several attempts by UN mediators as well as American, Soviet and other diplomats to bring the two sides together. Progress has been slow, but progress there has been. Since its involvement in the creation of the State of Israel, the UN has attempted to sponsor some diplomatic solution; it brokered a series of armistice talks and has policed the borders with Syria and Jordan. It has been the theatre of the battle between the two sides in the UN General Assembly as well as in the Security Council.

The Americans were as supportive of Arab countries as of Israel in the first decade after 1948. During the Suez invasion that Israel tried along with France and Britain, the USA was firmly against the three allies. It was after the 1967 and 1973 wars that the American line on Israel hardened. Outside Israel, America has the largest concentration of Jews and they have achieved status and prosperity there. Israel has cultivated American Jewry as its solid support in times of trouble. Even so, there have been many moves by the US to bring the two sides together.

The Camp David Accords of 1978 were a first step after the Yom Kippur War, which saw an Arab leader, Anwar Sadat of Egypt, willing to sit down with an Israeli prime minister, Menachem Begin, to do a deal. Later still the Oslo Accords were signed in 1993 by Yitzak Rabin and Shimon Peres with Yasser Arafat. Both Sadat and Rabin were assassinated by their own ungrateful peoples. The internal divisions within the Israeli nation between the left/Labour Party vision of Rabin and Peres and the right/Likud vision of Netanyahu and Sharon meant that after 1996 and Likud's coming to power, the Oslo Accords were sabotaged. President Clinton came very close in his 1998 Wye River Agreement, which he persuaded Netanyahu to sign, and later in his last days as president to reaching an agreement between Ehud Barak and Yasser Arafat. That was eight months before 9/11. Again, the Israeli electoral system, with its inability to create stable long-term majority governments, produced a swing from Barak to Sharon, from Labour to Likud.

George W. Bush's 'Road Map' was not a sudden response to 9/11, but another step in the long journey to resolve one of the most complex problems the world has faced. There is now the recognition for the legitimacy of the Palestinian demand for a state of their own. Israel's withdrawal from Gaza under the leadership of Sharon was a surprise, as it was bitterly fought by the illegal settlers. The election in spring 2006 saw the coalition of the new party, Kadima, with Labour. There was again hope that things would improve, but it was not to be.

The Palestinian national movement has also come a long way since its catastrophe (*al-Naqba*) in 1948. The PLO, formed in 1964, started as a liberation movement with a militant arm, like all liberation movements. It did after much struggle manage to sign the Oslo Accords and win a recognition for the right of Palestinians to exist as a state in their land. The PLO also conceded Israel's right to exist. Other groups such as Hezbollah and Hamas take a much more militant line on that issue. Israel in turn resorts to military attacks on Palestinian settlements as a counter-terrorist measure. Yet there is progress in a complex, slow and zigzagging way towards some sort of living together. Democratic elections for the Palestine Legislative Authority have advanced the debate further. The Palestine Authority has a democratically elected president in Abu Mazan.

The democratic election of Hamas as the majority party in Palestinian Legislative Assembly in January 2006 was a step forward. There was hope that Hamas would enter into the negotiating fold. True, Hamas is a liberation/terrorist organisation and did not concede Israel's right to exist, which was agreed to by the PLO at Oslo. Yet Hamas was forced by Abu Mazan to acknowledge the right of Israel to exist. But within days of that concession in July 2006, the militant wing of Hamas kidnapped an Israeli soldier while Hezbollah took two on the Israel–Lebanon border. Hostilities broke out on 12 July and lasted 34 days. A fragile ceasefire was imposed by the UN, but the future seems uncertain yet again. There is scope for change within all of us. It just takes a lot of patience and fortitude in face of attempts by hostile elements to wreck the progress. The Northern Ireland problem occupied much of the twentieth century for Britain, as it went through its ups and downs from the Easter 1916 Rising to the signing of the Good Friday Agreement in Easter 1998. Difficult problems of competing nationalisms can therefore be solved but not quickly.

What will not solve the problem is Bin Laden's insistence that Israel must be eliminated and that America and other Western powers must withdraw from the Middle East. For one thing, it is the Western powers (the European Union especially) which sustain the Palestinian Authority with their foreign aid. But, what is more, the right to land in the region will have to be shared by the two peoples whether we go back to the Torah or to the UN resolutions. Any solution has to accommodate the needs of both peoples; needs which have been forged in a history of injustice to both communities and will not be denied by force of one side or another.

Global Islamism and Anti-Semitism

The virulent anti-Israel and anti-Semitic tone of Global Islamism is not an accident. There was a tradition of tolerance of all faiths in Moorish Spain and in the caliphate, though all non-Islamic religious communities were treated as inferior to the Muslims. Christian anti-Semitism also has a long history and it is only in the second half of the twentieth century, after the tragic experience of the Holocaust, that one can say that it has been contained. The history of Arab Muslim anti-Semitism has a chapter in which the Mufti of

Jerusalem, Amin al-Husayni, collaborated with Goebbels in anti-Semitic propaganda. There was a growing struggle between Jews and Muslims in Palestine at this time and the Mufti banked on Hitler's victory – wrongly as it turned out.

Yet the similarity between National Socialism (Nazism) and Global Islamism is greater than just their virulent anti-Semitism. Nazism arose out of the defeat of the Central Powers, Germany and the Austro-Hungarian Habsburg Empire. Of course this happened at the same time as the defeat of the Ottoman Empire. Nazism was an ideology which asserted that Germans (Aryans) were a master race (*Herrenvolk*), but it had to explain how a master race could have lost in the First World War. The explanation was an external enemy, an Other that had stabbed the master race in the back. Such ideas were prevalent in Austria and in Germany in the aftermath of defeat in the First World War. Hitler wove them into an ideology. The resurgence of the master race then involved avenging the defeat at the hands of the Allied Powers – Britain, France, Russia and America – reversing the humiliation of the Treaty of Versailles, and it required the extermination of the alien, the Other, the Jew. It contained a moralistic critique of the effete races which had temporarily won against the master race by cunning and deceit. It had a superficial left-wing veneer inasmuch as National Socialism was anti-capitalist. But its main message was xenophobic. The Allies, it argued, were hypocritical and not to be trusted. The master race would rule the world and cleanse it of impurities, such as Jews, homosexuals, the disabled, blacks.

Replace the 'master race' with the chosen people, the followers of the Prophet, and the formulation of Global Islamism falls into place. It wants to defeat the enemy that has temporarily eclipsed the greatness of the Islamic Empire and of the Arab Muslims. But Muslims as a separate chosen people can reconquer and remove the enemy from their territories. All other religions are either subservient to Islam or they are false. They are impure and immoral, inferior to the master religion. Thus the intolerance of all others is given religious garb since Islam is the supreme and final truth given by the one and only God to his Final Messenger. The Jew is the common villain in both these ideologies, but also the West – the decadent, democratic West – is the enemy that has to be defeated. Homosexuals, drug addicts and all other decadent people are to be eliminated.

The Troublesome War against Terror

It is imperative in the light of such a reading that the critics of American and Western policies be separated from such a renegade ideology. To be anti-American has become fashionable in recent years, as it has been to be against imperialism in all its forms. The Western powers have conducted themselves in international affairs in a unilateral, bullying fashion. The legality of the invasion of Iraq was at best arguable since UN Resolution 1441 (along with the many others passed since the Iraqi invasion of Kuwait) was thought by many, even some American and British diplomats and lawyers, to be insufficient basis for an invasion. This is why a second UN resolution was sought. But the UN Security Council did not oblige. The weapons of mass destruction which were alleged to be the principal reason for the attack were not found either before or after the invasion. The argument that it was a humanitarian mission to save the Iraqis from a genocidal dictator was not made until the other explanations had proved false. The humanitarian argument was much more effective in the Balkan troubles when NATO was able to intervene without UN resolutions. But in the Balkan case, the ethnic cleansing was sudden and further atrocities were preventable. In the case of Saddam Hussein, the history of genocidal attacks on his own people was of long standing and well documented. No action had been taken against Saddam for many years and for a while, during the Iran–Iraq war of 1980–88, he was seen as an ally on the cynical ground that my enemy's enemy is my friend. So the idea that the US and the UK were invading Saddam for humanitarian reasons did not convince.

The invasion faced a lot of opposition around the world and is still the subject of debate. The proponents of the war argue that Iraq is now a democracy with a parliament in which the major sectarian groups are represented; despite much mayhem wrought by the terrorists, it has a democratic regime with an all-party national government. Peace will not be easy or quick. The age-old divisions between the Shi'a and the Sunni are constantly on the boil even as the two groups are represented in the parliament. There is also the tricky question of Kurdish autonomy. All these divisions were ruthlessly suppressed by Saddam Hussein when he was in power. But that repression gave Iraq a false gloss of order and stability. The livelihood of the marsh Arabs, most of them Shi'a, was destroyed by the draining of the marshes under Saddam's orders. It is in comparison to that Iraq that one has to judge present-day Iraq, the supporters of the war argue. Even post-war West Germany took four years before Konrad Adenauer became its chancellor and stability could be assured. Iraq is yet only three years from the war. But while the outcome could be good eventually, the process of getting there leaves a lot to be criticised.

There has also been a sea change in the attitude of the Western powers, especially the USA and the UK, concerning the legal defences against terrorism. The 9/11 events shocked the American public and indeed the American government. The passing of the Patriot Act was the immediate response. A Department of Homeland Security was created. The USA now regards itself as at war with the terrorists. It interprets this literally, like a war against sovereign states, while it is actually global guerrilla warfare with a scattered and decentralised enemy. At the same time it has avoided being caught by the Geneva and other conventions on the treatment of war prisoners. It has captured soldiers in Afghanistan, and indeed at home, whom it has treated as if they are enemy combatants. There are people urging America to be tougher on terrorists while there is also a strong voice increasingly inside America and a much louder voice outside that is critical of the government's methods. The creation of the Guantánamo Bay prison for interrogating alleged terrorists outside American territorial jurisdiction has attracted much criticism. It is a gross violation of human rights by any description. The US Supreme Court finally questioned the powers of the US government to defy the Geneva Conventions in the summer of 2006. Further, there is now evidence that the American government spied on its citizens without adequate safeguards such as permission from the courts to invade privacy. Thus, while fighting terrorists, the war has extended to all citizens. This may be required but only if it is within the rule of law.

The US policy has been recently described in trenchant terms as follows:

What unites the Bush Administration's obsession with, on the one hand, the old model of war against states and, on the other, the use of new 'preventive paradigm' at home and abroad is an almost total contempt for the importance of maintaining legitimacy in the struggle against terrorism.[40]

Of course, the policy is carried out by a democratically elected government, with the president re-elected in face of all the criticism of his policy on Iraq and his policy on the war against terrorism. Even so, there is a gap between legality and legitimacy and the claims of liberal modernity (which is being defended against the attacks by Global Islamism) have to be admitted. The acts in Iraq and in Guantánamo will never be legitimate in the eyes of many people, but at least they should be judged for their legality. There is a legal process which can bring these miscreants to justice; examples of torture and other violations of human rights can be exposed.[41] Privates in the American army have been tried and, where found guilty, punished. If there are superior officers as yet unpunished despite their complicity in the Abu Ghraib atrocities, the process of open information will no doubt get at them. Americans have a fine tradition of fighting for civil liberties, especially against the actions of the Executive, and one trusts that this tradition has sufficient strength left to bring their own Executive to book. But that presumes a continuation of the rule of law and an open liberal democratic society, not the intolerant monopolistic monotheism that Bin Laden preaches. Anti-Americanism and anti-imperialism have to be distanced from Global Islamism, which is parasitical on these sentiments.

The British response to terrorism has been no less controversial but has gone through a much more thorough legislative scrutiny.

British legislation on terrorism predates 9/11 since it started with the troubles in Northern Ireland. But post 9/11, the government did try to detain some foreign terrorist suspects. The highest judicial court in Britain, the Appellate Committee of the House of Lords, judged their detention to be in breach of the European Convention of Human Rights (which is now a part of British law since the Labour government incorporated it upon coming to power). The grounds were that the government had detained foreigners and not British suspects; thus this was discrimination on grounds of nationality. The government had to quickly pass a Prevention of Terrorism Bill through two houses of Parliament in which many safeguards were incorporated to make quite sure that if there was going to be detention without a trial the government sought permission from the courts. The need for new laws is still there but there is also a legislative process of debate and scrutiny plus an independent judiciary, which gives some hope for legitimacy as well as legality.

The dilemma for governments is acute. The global terrorism phenomenon is unprecedented inasmuch as it is global and armed with the latest electronic and armaments technology. It is also a guerrilla war in which the enemy can be anywhere. The multiracial character of modern Western societies and the freedom and rights that all residents enjoy make it difficult to identify who the terrorist may be among the population. It is of course impossible to arrest a suicide bomber after he has committed his crime, but he is difficult to arrest before the crime, in the absence of solid evidence. So the problem is that a balance has to be struck between two probabilities. The fierce guardian of human rights would like to avoid any chance that an innocent person is incarcerated and denied his or her civil liberties. The anti-terrorist is keen to avoid any chance that a likely bomber will escape undetected and blow civilians up causing injury and death. Of course the two could be the same person. So a balance has to be struck and the rule of law has to be obeyed. There will be always disputes about the behaviour of governments in fighting terrorists, but inasmuch as the fight is to preserve a way of life – peaceful, tolerant and democratic – there has to be vigilance.

The obverse side of the coin of fighting terrorism (not just the terrorists) is to question whether the way in which its global appeal is made cannot be subjected to the same sort of scrutiny as we do with our own conduct. Is Global Islamism truthful in its claims?

Deconstructing Global Islamism

A beginning has also to be made in deconstructing the ideology of Global Islamism so far as Muslims are concerned. Thus the notion that Global Islamism speaks for the *umma* has to be disabused. This is partly because there is no such single *umma*. It is a construct which had some reality in the days when the Muslims were a single community and lived closely together. That lasted about thirty years at most after the death of the Prophet, and those years were marked by conflict and civil war for the succession to the caliphate in the *umma*. Two out of the first four caliphs were murdered. The community split between Sunni and Shi'a precisely because there was a doctrinal dispute about the legitimacy of the criteria for succession to the caliphate. By the time the Umayyad dynasty took over, what existed was an empire won by the sword and ruled by a king. The king claimed a connection with the Prophet but this was increasingly tenuous. The caliph had no spiritual qualifications necessarily and held the community together by conquest. The succession of caliphates in Damascus, Baghdad and Istanbul were not spiritual kingdoms but just temporal powers won by the might of military arms.[42]

In fact, within the traditions of a single Book and single Prophet, Islam flourished in different parts of the world by adapting to local cultures and religions. There was and is no single Church or clergy with any spiritual hierarchical authority. As indicated above, Christendom in the fifteenth century had perhaps greater reality, though the Eastern Church had gone its own way and the pope only ruled over the Western Church. Even so, there was heresy, and the Holy Inquisition was required to assert the authority of the pope. The Muslim *umma* is a post-modern reconstruction resulting from the revival of Wahhabism. Since this sect takes Muslims back to the simpler days of the Prophet's time, it can pretend that Muslims form an *umma* as once they did. Those old days when the Prophet's Companions ruled after his death, are hardly ideal, as we have seen. Even if they had been as good as some people claim, it is irrelevant. The billion and a quarter Muslims who live and pray as Muslims do it in their own separate ways. Most of them do not follow the Wahhabi way and are no more a single body than Christians are. Of course, with globalisation, there is increased communication and an awareness of shared history, largely through the diasporas which bring together Muslims of various ethnicities in many Western countries. The tradition of free speech and free association that these countries' citizens have won over decades of struggle are useful to Muslims to organise politically, even as some hope to reject the very liberal freedoms they use. But that is their right, as it is the right of various Leninist sects that reject liberal capitalist democracy and agitate for its overthrow via the revolution.

Globalisation makes it possible for Muslims to arrive at a situation in which it could be an aspiration to realise such an *umma*, if a leader can be found who can acquire the spiritual authority and persuasive powers to do so. Bin Laden aspires to be such a leader; he may even think he is such a leader, although Muslims around the world will hardly entertain his claim. For one thing, he does not believe in healing the historic wound to the original *umma* caused by the Sunni–Shi'a split. Indeed, so far as I am aware, there is no ecumenical movement within Islam to achieve such a unity. But even if another leader came and united the community (and this is very unlikely), such an *umma* would be a spiritual not a political community.

Are (Arab) Muslims in Historical Decline?

The historical eclipse of the Muslims as a single political power is a fact. But, then, so have other nations – British, French, Belgian, Spanish, Dutch, Japanese – lost their empires. The question is: has there been a decline of Muslims, in Arabia especially, in fact – or is it only a perception? So far as I am aware, no single account has been made of the standards of living, incomes and human development levels of Muslims as compared to non-Muslims. What we do have is measures of these variables by individual countries where Muslims live. We can only go by broad indicators.

The countries in Arabia are in a middle-income rather than low-income range by international standards, richer than Africa and South Asia, if not Southeast Asia as well. The United Nations Development Programme (UNDP) has published a *Human Development Report* since 1990. It publishes a Human Development Index (HDI) which summarises three measures of well-being – longevity, literacy and access to resources as measured by income per capita (in purchasing power parity units to make international comparisons easier). For each of the three dimensions measures are calibrated to lie between 0 and 1, with one representing the highest achievable level. The three separate measures are then combined in an overall measure, also lying between 0 and 1, which gives us the HDI. Countries are also ranked from 1 to 177 by their HDI score, with 1 for the country with the highest HDI. In the UN *Human Development Report* of 2004, countries are divided into three categories – High human development (0.8 and above), Medium human development (0.5 to 0.8) and Low human development (below 0.5).

Arab countries do not do badly in terms of HDI. In the High category are Bahrain (40), Kuwait (44), Qatar (47), UAE (49); the figure in parentheses indicates their rank in terms of Human Development Index among 177 countries. In the Middle category are Libya (58), Oman (74), Saudi Arabia (77), Lebanon (80), Jordan (90), Tunisia (92), Iran (101), Occupied Palestine Territories (102), Syria (106), Algeria (108), Egypt (120), Morocco (125). Only Yemen (149) is in the low category. Among non-Arab Muslim countries Brunei (33) is among the High and Malaysia (59), Bosnia (66), Turkey (88), Indonesia (111), Bangladesh (138) are all in the Medium category, and only Pakistan (142) is in the Low category.

The UNDP published an *Arab Human Development Report* in 2002, and has published further reports on the Arab region. Its conclusions are that Arab countries need to improve their knowledge base, reduce the gender disparity in their societies and improve political representation. The future of Arab human development is of course in Arab hands, but the need is to grasp the challenge of modernisation using the instruments of knowledge, realise the full potential of women as well as men, and work towards a democratisation of the region. These are modern responses to contemporary challenges, and do not involve going back twelve hundred years to some simple society.

Thus while some may perceive that there may be a political decline as an ex-empire, neither the countries of the Middle East, nor elsewhere where the bulk of the Muslim population lives, can be characterised as severely deprived, relative to the Third World as a whole. This is not to say they are developed countries or that there is no poverty among them. But in this they are no different to many other countries, many of them ex-colonies. In terms of women's relative position in human development, the Gender-related Development Index of the UNDP singles out Saudi Arabia, Pakistan, Oman, Syria, Yemen as countries whose women fare relatively worse than the average population in terms of human development indices. Here four out of five are in the Arab region. Adult illiteracy rates are also high among these countries, reflecting female illiteracy. Thus among those countries that have high adult illiteracy rates are Bahrain, Kuwait, Qatar, Libya, Lebanon, Malaysia, which all have illiteracy rates higher than 10 per cent; the United Arab Emirates, Oman, Saudi Arabia, Tunisia, Iran, Syria, Algeria and Indonesia, which all have illiteracy rates higher than 20 per cent; and Egypt, Morocco, Bangladesh, Sudan, Pakistan and Yemen, where illiteracy rates are higher than 40 per cent. Thus education is a gaping hole in many of these societies.

There are, of course, very few democracies among the Arab countries (Lebanon is an exception), though there are other Muslim countries – Malaysia, Bangladesh, Indonesia – which are democratic. Pakistan has had a mixed experience of roughly half the years it has been independent as a democracy and half under military dictatorship. Egypt is slowly tending towards democracy and Iraq has had successful democratic elections. Recent elections for the Palestine Legislative Assembly produced a real surprise when Hamas came through as the majority party. Thus Islam is compatible with democracy as well as the decent treatment of women. What is required is the pursuit of economic and human development with a good gender-oriented policy and good governance via a democratic polity.

The story of Arab Muslims and other Muslims in this sense is not different from that of many other people. Thus, while there are poor people, unequal incomes, women facing discrimination and an income level short of the developed country level, there cannot be any excuse for regarding Muslims as permanently deprived. Inasmuch as some Muslims are deprived, the key to their emancipation is in their hands as they need to follow sensible policies in terms of education of their children, especially of girls, devote more resources to health, encourage enterprise and competition, invest in research and development and run responsible macroeconomic policies. These are the ingredients all countries need to follow if they are to grow and achieve higher levels of human development and equity. Muslims anywhere and everywhere can be as well off as anyone else; the key is in their hands, not in anyone else's.

Bin Laden's argument has therefore got to be about the fact that there is no longer a Muslim empire, and that there are non-

Muslim countries which are powerful. It is a reluctance to face change as others have done, and also to face the stark truth that among Muslims there are serious differences as to what is proper political and moral conduct. There is diversity and plurality. He is set against such diversity and wishes there were a single monolithic religious regime which all obey. Such an empire would be a nightmare not just for non-Muslims but for many Muslims as well. Osama's Taliban friends demonstrated this on a small scale when they ran an Islamic regime in Afghanistan which drove women indoors and deprived them of education or any chance of working outside their homes, punished minorities, publicly executed small-time criminals and destroyed the world-historic statues of the Buddha at Bamiyan.

In this matter, Bin Laden is superficially like the seventeenth-century English Puritans, who also wished the world was simpler and obeyed the simplicities they had derived from the Bible. Yet the Puritans were respectful of individuality and of the right to debate and discuss. As they settled in America, the Puritans laid the foundations of fine democratic practices in their local communities and a refusal to obey laws that they had not given their assent to. It is out of such creative potential of religious dissent that material and intellectual developments since then have made the West prosperous, liberal, sceptical, rational and democratic. There has been a long struggle against the yoke of religion in daily life as well as for a separation of Church and State. This struggle was waged by every sector of society, and democracy grew in the crucible of such struggles. Religious discrimination against Catholics, non-Anglican Christians and Jews was routine in England and it took all of the nineteenth century to remove the handicaps placed on all non-Anglican worshippers. Atheists had their battles, as the example of Charles Bradlaugh MP shows: he was repeatedly denied entry to the House of Commons despite winning elections, because he refused to swear an oath of allegiance. The winning of freedom from the rule of one sect and one religion has been invaluable for the flowering of democracy and decency.

The same struggle has been waged in the twentieth century for the civil rights of minorities defined by race or ethnicity – blacks and Native Americans in the USA and ethnic minorities everywhere else in the West. Homosexuals have won hard-fought rights in many (alas not all) Western countries to pursue the lifestyle they desire. Women have come a long way in their fight for equality but there is still some way to go. People with disabilities were despised and gassed by the Nazis. They were also severely neglected in many societies. Again, to treat them as equal to all the rest is a democratic struggle.

In the course of these developments religion itself has become more tolerant in the West. The routine anti-Semitism of the Christian Churches is now a thing of the past. The prejudice against women clergy is eroding slowly. There is an acceptance by the Anglican Church at least of homosexuality as a natural trait, yet there are differences as to whether clergy can be homosexuals. Religion does not divide; nor is it harnessed to the state's war efforts as was usual until recently.

In a famous sentence in his preface to *Capital* Volume 1, Marx wrote '*De Te Fabula Naratur*' – It is your story which is being told. He meant that future developments in Germany would take the same path as in England. He was right in the long run, though there were twists and turns before Germany took a liberal democratic path as Britain had done. This will also be the story of the Muslims. Global Islamism as a fascist, intolerant programme of asserting a monolithic monopoly of puritanical Islam will lose. Material and intellectual developments will take place in the Muslim world, as they have for other communities. These developments will divert attention away from the victim mentality that Global Islamism cultivates and feeds on. Muslims will continue to add to the diversity of life around the world.

Defeating Global Islamism

The real challenge is not just to understand why Global Islamism appeals to many Muslim young people, deconstructing it so that its pretensions are exposed for all to see, but eventually to defeat it and its capacity for immense violence and intolerance. It has to be defeated as much for the sake of Muslims and their ability to lead lives of their choice in the country of their choice as for the rest of us who also want to do the same. Inasmuch as Global Islamism is an ideology, we need to ask whether there are any lessons to be learnt from the way in which we combated Communism.

It is ultimately Communism rather than Nazism that is the appropriate example for us to study. Nazism does share many characteristics with Global Islamism, as we saw above, including anti-Semitism and the notion of a chosen people. But Nazism derived its strength from the capture of power in a modern developed economy and the harnessing of its industrial capacity for military preparation. It did not try to win over the hearts and minds even of the German people, much less the rest of the world. Nazism was short-lived – some 12 years in power and 25 years between Hitler's

Beer Hall putsch and his death in the bunker. It was an extremely vile ideology; it chose to take on the world's military powers openly and lost. Global Islamism relies on the hearts and minds of Muslim youth which make it able to conduct a guerrilla war with limited investment in armies and armaments. It is primarily about sowing ideas in the minds of Muslim youth so that they will be incited to act in a violent manner. It is not the Second World War that we have to fight again, but a longer and more protracted battle in which ideas are as important as armaments.

The Second World War was a war in which Communism collaborated with liberal democracies to destroy Nazism. Whatever the defects of Communism as it later developed in Russia, it is not a racist creed. It was after the war that the battle against Communism was waged and it took 45 years to defeat. Communism was fought militarily in a Cold War with round-the-clock preparedness for waging war, with troops stationed around the world encircling the perimeter of the Communist world. But in the course of those 45 years, Communism spread and its influence grew. The most populous country in the world, China, joined the Soviet Union after the Second World War and then along came North Korea, North Vietnam and Cambodia – all in Asia. Eastern European countries were swallowed up by Communism according to the implicit understanding of 'spheres of influence' in a post-war settlement. Then Cuba and Ethiopia became formally Communist.

Communism also made inroads in the higher education institutions in Europe and in America. Social sciences were much influenced by Marxism and Communism. Marx's manuscripts were retrieved, translated and published. The history of socialism was studied critically and very soon debates broke out on the left as to whether the Soviet version of Marxism was the valid one. Out of this ferment came the New Left, which was a critique of Western societies to begin with but also went on to defy the Communist orthodoxies. There was much to be gained by allowing free inquiry into Marxism, if only in deglamorising the Soviet Union as a Marxist haven. This is what liberal democratic society can do best: allow the free flow of information and debate and the criticism of all ideas. Why not try it with Global Islamism?

Of course, the analogy with Global Islamism is not and cannot be exact. After all is said and done, Communism is a modernist philosophy. It is a quarrel within the Enlightenment tradition. Marx was a revolutionary humanist wedded to reason and freedom in his way. Even the later distortions of Leninism did not make Communism reject modernity. It charted an alternative economic path for development and used non-democratic, indeed authoritarian, means to achieve its aims. Yet, as stated, Communism retains a lot of appeal still since it is non-exclusive and offers hope to the poor and the deprived. Global Islamism is an excluding ideology since all non-Muslims are anathema for it and it rejects all aspects of modernity (though it feels free to criticise the West for not living up to the ideals of the Enlightenment). The similarity is that both are anti-American and anti-imperialist, yet also with ambitions of hegemonic domination.

Communism in its battle against the West fought a cultural war as much as a military one. The West saw this early on and retaliated. Thus Communism posed the contrast of people's democracies with the bourgeois democracies, the positive economic rights enjoyed by its people with the merely negative rights of civil liberty enjoyed by Western citizens. Communism could point to the racism and the discrimination suffered by American blacks or the subjects of the empires of Western imperial powers. It was alert to all violations of human rights by Western governments whether at home or abroad. Thus police brutality and military atrocities were always highlighted when civil demonstrations were put down in the democracies.

The West retaliated in two main ways: by turning the tables on Communism and by mounting a critique of the constant violations of citizens' rights in the Communist countries. Their efforts received a great boost when Khrushchev made his de-Stalinisation speech in 1956 at the Twentieth Party Congress. Once the gulag was associated with Communism, the advantage Communism had over liberal democracies began to vanish. Here was an admission from the home team, as it were, that things were rotten in the Soviet Union just as its worst enemies had been saying. For many Communists round the world this was a shock, and the Communist movement internationally never recovered its original idealistic gloss.

This battle was fought along cultural lines as much as along propaganda and political lines. Thus the Communists always displayed their artistic supporters prominently – Pablo Picasso, Paul Robeson, Jean-Paul Sartre. The West got disillusioned Communists to write up their experiences to warn other likely converts of what Communism was really like. *The God that Failed* was the book to which famous authors such as Ignazio Silone, and Arthur Koestler contributed and which was widely distributed at subsidised prices by the Americans. The Communists had international congresses for artists and writers where the converted performed and the innocent were converted. The West had its Congress for Cultural Freedom, which also tried to entice intellectuals, writers and artists to join the liberal cause. A magazine, *Encounter*, was financed covertly by the CIA; it was co-edited by the British poet Stephen Spender and received contributions from some of the best writers worldwide. It also paid well since it was well financed.[43] Modern opera and abstract art were as generously financed as intellectual writing in this battle.

The idea was that it is the literate and the articulate elite that is crucial to the battle of ideas and it is the elite that has to be moved to change sides or stick to the side they are already on and not be seduced by the other side. The elite were enticed not by crude transparent propaganda, but by high art and good argument, where they could view the benefits of freedom.

Meanwhile, the West also cleaned up its act. It made great strides in anti-racism, in human rights, in decolonisation, in promoting economic development in the developing world. Much of this was a result of the struggle by the groups who had the most to gain from such freedoms, but it was shrewd politicians like Harold Macmillan who could discern 'the winds of change' blowing across Africa and demanding decolonisation. John F. Kennedy harnessed the idealism of American youth in launching the Peace Corps, though his Alliance for Freedom for Latin America was less of a success. But the important thing was to encourage and admit change and criticism. Communism appealed to the idealism of the young, so there had to be a rival story that was equally appealing.

The West kept on making mistakes, as in Vietnam. Yet the fury it unleashed in the USA itself among the young, and abroad in the 1968 student 'troubles', could not be harnessed by the orthodox

Communists since it had a libertarian ethos. The students were against the suppression of the Czech rebellion in the Prague Spring of 1968 as they were against de Gaulle or Lyndon Johnson. The hypocrisy of the Communist regimes, which rolled out guns and tanks against civilians within their empire while criticising the slightest deviation from good behaviour on the part of the West, became clear to everyone. What the young people saw was that their own system in the West, warts and all, was better than the alternative.

The biggest battle was in the economic sphere, of course. Communism had the declared ambition of overtaking capitalism in the material production of goods and services. It criticised capitalism for its waste and inefficiencies, its unemployment and trade cycles, its inequalities of income and poverty amidst plenty, and so on. Ultimately, through 25 years of Keynesian full employment and growth, and despite the stagflation caused by the oil price rise, the Western democracies came through with their economies more productive and raising living standards faster than could the Soviet Union.[44]

Today the challenge of Communism in the economic sphere has mutated into the movement against globalisation. Many of the themes recur – the inefficiencies and inequities of free markets, the wastefulness of unemployment, the asymmetry of economic power of the rich nations against the poor ones. Of course Communism is no longer backed by the military power which made it so sinister for its own citizens. Thus, with its incubus gone, its better side, critical of the economic frailties of capitalism, come to the fore. But the answer to that will be, as it always was, in reforming economic policies so that they best combine efficiency and equity while preserving innovative activity and diversity of choice. It is not a battle that will end, but there has been one major transformation since the early years of the last century. There are today no alternatives to capitalism; the debate is about what type of capitalism one wants. Communism as an alternative economic system has bitten the dust.

There is no viable economic challenge from Global Islamism. In the hypothetical case of Bin Laden or some other Global Islamist coming to power in Saudi Arabia, oil price volatility would increase. There are, however, always other sources of supplies and substitution possibilities. This was the lesson learnt from the two oil shocks of the 1970s. The greater challenge is cultural, and it is confined to the hearts and minds of Muslims. But since Global Islamism rejects modernity and asserts the power of orthodox fundamentalism, the response has to be to expose its orthodox pretensions and at the same time show that there is a lot in modernity which is consistent with Islam. There was once, about a thousand years ago, a lively debating tradition among Muslim philosophers when orthodoxies were challenged and had to be justified by reason. After that, during the second millennium CE, there seems to have been stagnation in the field of critical debate within Islam. There was a modernising movement in Islam through the middle nineteenth century until the late twentieth century. Its recent retreat needs to be challenged and reversed, by asserting that Muslims around the world, whether living in Muslim majority countries or elsewhere, have led lives which have fruitfully combined religion and modernity.[45]

We also need much wider support for studies of Islam and Muslim culture. Very much as Marxism was taken up in higher education institutions in the post-war period, we need many more people, non-Muslims as well as Muslims, to study Islam. Thus the kind of textual study of the Bible that has gone on since the middle of the nineteenth century at least has not taken off in the case of the Qur'an, though there are some scholars who do plough their lonely furrow in this field.[46] This will allow us to read the Qur'an not only as a holy book but as a historical document, a product of a specific time and culture, much as the Bible is. Such an expansion of Islamic studies by scholars trained in modern methods of research may illuminate many hitherto hidden aspects of Islam just as the new translations of Marx's work altered our picture of his theories. We have to remove the excessive and uncritical religiosity with which the Qur'an is treated even by non-Muslims. This is designed not to belittle or insult Islam but to treat it on a par with the other great religions of the world.

Take the controversy about the cartoons which raged across countries in the early months of 2006. Certain aspects are crucial. There is on the one hand freedom of speech, and even those who carry placards 'Death to Freedom of Speech' ironically assert its importance. But more than that the question is, what are the rules about portrayal of the Prophet in Islam? There is, as mentioned earlier, no Qur'anic injunction against it. There are coins and portraits in existence from centuries ago. It should be possible to mount a proper exhibition of archival material – coins, manuscripts, paintings and statuary – to display the changing practice over the centuries.

There is every reason not to accept the idea that Islam has been timeless, as the Islamists claim today, or that practices about head covering or women's rights in current orthodoxies have any support in doctrine or indeed even in common sense. The treatment that the Taliban meted out to Afghan women during their brief rule was a throwback to some medieval past, yet hardly true to the history of women in Islam. There are dynamic women leaders in Muslim history, women who ruled, and who made fortunes in trade (Khadija, the Prophet's first wife) and who led armies (Ayesha, another of the Prophet's wives) and discussed theology (Salamah, another of the Prophet's wives), and who today are lawyers, politicians, fashion designers, musicians. It is their stories which need to be retrieved against the Islamist insistence on the invisibility of women to the outside world. Our knowledge of Islam has to be made deep as well as critical so that we can judge the Islamists for what they are – people who substitute their opinion, but recently formulated, as age-old orthodoxy.

The rest of us – non-Muslims – also need to claim the thousand years of Islamic art and sculpture, architecture and music as our heritage as much as that of Muslims. In India, for example, the classical musical tradition is syncretic: cultural forms are shared by Muslims and Hindus. Classical vocalists sing Hindu devotional songs – *bhajan*s – just as willingly as Hindu classical vocalists sing *qawwali*s, which are sung in shrines. The sufi tradition has suffused the music of both communities. Urdu *ghazal*s, Persian poetry, Arabic romances are all part of the heritage that many people enjoy in the Indian subcontinent and among diasporas around the world. After all, Aladdin and his magic lamp, Sinbad and other stories from the *Arabian Nights*, the poems of Rumi, the music of Nusrat Fateh Ali Khan, the beauty of the Taj Mahal and the Alhambra, the travelogue of Ibn Batuta – these are all our common heritage.

We need to do the same with the religion. As an atheist who has lived in the West, I can recite the Lord's Prayer (having heard Joan Baez sing it) and am familiar with the Gospels and perhaps a few parts of the Old Testament. I treat them as pieces of literature not religion. The Bible has been so superbly translated into English in the King James version that many think Jesus spoke in English.[47] The Qur'an is a classic of Arabic language; when one hears it recited it has mesmeric qualities even though you don't understand a word of it (as, indeed, many non-Arabic-speaking Muslims don't). But the available English translations of the Qur'an (at least the few that I have read) do not have memorable lines; even the first seven *shura*s of the Qur'an are unknown to many of us who would recognise the Lord's Prayer. Is it not a worthy cultural project for someone or several people to undertake to produce a poetic translation of the Qur'an which can be recited or even sung?

The issue here is not Islam as a religion or the Qur'an as a holy book. The issue is the integration of Muslim culture into other cultures around the world, just as Western culture has been absorbed by everyone. Globalisation presents the opportunity for us to sample the best of the world's cultures. Indeed we may be on the brink of creating a global culture to which every culture will contribute; along the way these cultures will themselves change and integrate better with each other. After two hundred years of economic domination by the West, there are for the first time serious challenges from Asia – China, South Korea, Japan and India. The West is being forced to compete to retain its jobs: witness the panic measures against the outsourcing of jobs to India or the resistance in Europe and the USA to the takeover of Western companies by Asian ones. The West is learning about other cultures, if only to be able to sell its wares better in the new and growing markets. Globalisation is a story which can genuinely alter the mental map of economic power that we have carried with us for decades. The new century holds real promise for many countries that have been in the position of supplicant and victim in the past. Muslims are no exception to this. A glance at the dynamic economy of Malaysia, with its majority Muslim population, shows how well an economy can grow.

Muslims will assimilate and integrate in whichever societies they choose to live if they are in a minority. But their feelings of exclusion and isolation are heightened by our ignorance of their culture. It is part of the power of Global Islamism to play on that isolation and sharpen it into a tool suffused with anger and a feeling of rejection. It then tells the young Muslim man and woman that it will always be thus, since the ignorance of their culture arises from the arrogance of the West, an arrogance that has been visited upon the Muslims for the last hundred years. This is where the rest of us need to assimilate and absorb elements of Muslim culture – the music, the poetry, the calligraphy, the cuisine – in our own lives. Our isolation has to be broken down, as much as that of the Muslims living in our midst.

Conclusion

Global Islamism can be understood, analysed and combated. As an ideology of Muslim emancipation, it is regressive, intolerant and racist. Muslims do not need it since its recipe for Muslim progress is backward-looking and exclusionist. Neither the 1.5 billion Muslims in the world nor the 4.5 billion non-Muslims need its murderous habits to be around much longer. If it is seen as an ideology rather than a religion, Global Islamism can be shrunk to its proper size and fought – as other ideologies have been fought before.

SIX

Winning the War against Terrorism

The new terrorism is different from what we have known for a long time. Even though it has now lasted for more than a dozen years (since the first attempt, in February 1993, to bomb the World Trade Center in New York), many people still deny its novelty. They argue that one man's terrorist is another's liberation fighter. However, liberation struggles are for a nationalist cause, often against an imperial power, and the aim has been confined to winning independence for the nation. Nevertheless, we were told that Nelson Mandela was a terrorist by no less a person than Margaret Thatcher. Bin Laden, though, is not Mandela. Mandela's struggle was anti-racist and was for equality for his people in their own home against their white fellow countrymen.

People point out, quite rightly, that in the war on terror America has committed gross violations of human rights. Yet there is a better than evens chance that legal processes will try to pin the blame where it belongs, so long as what has happened is illegal. The reason one can say this with confidence is that, even when Western governments have made mistakes and violated human rights, there has always been someone in the country, often an ordinary citizen or even an ambitious district attorney, who has pursued the erring government in court. Even as long ago as the 1780s, with the East India Company's rule barely established in Bengal, the governor-general, Warren Hastings was responsible for acts which led to a process in the British Parliament to impeach him. Edmund Burke took the lead in the trial. Hastings was acquitted, but the trial was what distinguished British rule from all that went before. The atrocities Hastings was alleged to have committed were the staple diet of intrigues within India's warring princely families. Whereas none of them ever faced a trial, Hastings did.

This is what I call liberal modernity. It is not that mistakes have not been made in the fight against terrorism but that the mistakes are corrigible. The process is open and legal redress is available. By contrast, what Bin Laden poses as his solution to all problems is an unquestioning submission to his views about the state of Muslims, laced with the words of the holy book as interpreted by him. That is if you are a Muslim. If you are not, you either convert to Islam or go under. His version of international law says that Indonesia had every right to take over East Timor and that Iraq should not have been attacked for invading Kuwait. His morality says that the Torah gives Muslims every right to to take over the land in dispute in Palestine since God was originally and at all times the God of Muslims; Jews and Christians are just imperfect versions of the perfection that Muslims are.

It is not just that Bin Laden's ideas are idiosyncratic. They have murderous consequences. The victims of his attacks are not selected; they are all people who reside in any part of the world where

Westerners holiday (Bali) or work (New York, London), or where they are supposed to have influence (Madrid) or where Muslims have a dispute with fellow Muslims or non-Muslims (Delhi, Mumbai). His war has only one aim: defeat for non-Muslims wherever they are, and if Muslims also get killed in the process that is just too bad.

Osama Bin Laden is not crazy; nor is he demented. He is a genius of global guerrilla warfare and a superb rhetorician who has built a worldwide loose coalition of terrorist cells staffed by young men and women who are willing to kill and die for him. We need to understand why his ideas have such power and what we can do to counter the fact so that we can save not just ourselves but also those eager men and women from themselves.

This is what this book has tried to do. It has described Bin Laden's ideology in some detail, put it in the context of the twentieth-century history of the Middle East and the longer history of Muslims, drawn parallels with other ideologies and derived lessons from previous struggles against these ideologies. It has 'desacrilised' the message of Global Islamism as being not of a religious nature but of an ideology.

To paraphrase the words of Karl Marx's eleventh thesis on Feuerbach: 'We have tried to interpret Global Islamism; the task however is to defeat it.'

Notes

1. Samuel Huntington, 'The Clash of Civilizations?' *Foreign Affairs*, Summer 1993, *The Clash of Civilizations and the Remaking of the World Order*, Simon & Schuster, New York, 1996. Among his early critics see Fred Halliday, *Islam and the Myth of Confrontation: Religion and Politics in the Middle East*, I.B. Tauris, London, 1995. Amartya Sen has recently also criticised Huntington in *The Argumentative Indian: Writings on Indian History, Culture and Identity*, Allen Lane, London, 2005.

2. 'In 66/685f, the first known coin identifying Muhammad as rasul Allah (messenger of God) was struck at Bishapur in Fars by a pro-Zubayrid governor, and in 71/690f. the message was repeated on another Arab-Sassanian dirham struck at the same place, this time by a supporter of the Umayyads.' Patricia Crone and Martin Hinds, *God's Caliph*, Cambridge University Press, Cambridge, 1986, p. 25.

3. There is a vast literature on the Russian Revolution. See Meghnad Desai, *Marx's Revenge: The Resurgence of Capitalism and the Death of Statist Socialism*, Verso, London, 2002.

4. There are many references. See among others François Furet, *The Passing of an Illusion*, University of Chicago Press, Chicago, 1999; Jung Chang and Jon Halliday, *Mao: The Unknown Story*, Jonathan Cape, London, 2005; Stephane Courtois et al., *The Black Book of Communism*, Harvard University Press, Cambridge MA, 1999.

5. In his first broadcast of 2006 and one after a long interval of over a year since the previous one, Osma Bin Laden offered to negotiate with his enemies. His offer was summarily rejected by Dick Cheney, the American vice-president.

6. Huntington, 'The Clash of Civilizations?'

7. An example of the debate among the Muslims is Irshad Manji, *The Trouble with Islam Today: A Wakeup Call to Honesty and Change*, Mainstream Publishing, London, 2005.

8. By 'Muslim countries' I mean countries with a Muslim majority population. There are also countries with a Muslim minority population such as India with 144 million Muslims, larger than all but one Muslim country, Indonesia. Of all the countries where the Muslims are in a majority, only four can be labelled Islamic – Saudi Arabia, Iran, Somalia and Sudan. On Islamism, see Olivier Roy, *The Failure of Political Islam*, Harvard Univrsity Press, Cambridge MA 1994; and *Globalised Islam: The Search for a New Ummah*, C. Hurst, London, 2005.

9. For a comprehensive history, see Peter Marshall, *Demanding the Impossible: A History of Anarchism*, HarperCollins, London, 1992.

10. For the early history of the caliphate, see Mahmoud Ayoub, *The Crisis of Muslim History: Religion and Politics in Early Islam*, One World, Oxford, 2003. There is dispute about the status of Ali as the Umayyad Caliphs who displaced him in a civil war claim that he was a pretender while for Shi'a he is an imam and a martyr.

11. Ruddock Mackay, *Balfour: Intellectual Statesman*, Oxford University Press, Oxford, 1985.

12. Crone and Hinds, *God's Caliph*, p. 33, quoting an eighth-century authority, Jarir bin Atiyya bin al-Khatafa. Despite this status, Crone and Hinds argue that the Caliphs lost their religious as against their secular authority when the caliphate became dynastic and went from one family to another. It still does not affect the notion that the caliphate was central to Muslim perceptions.

13. Muhammad Iqbal, *Shikwa and Jawab-e-Shikwa: Iqbal's Dialogue with Allah*, trans. and introduced by Khushwant Singh, Oxford University Press, Delhi, 1981. All quotations are indicated by page numbers of this edition.

14. Albert Hourani, *A History of the Arab Peoples*, Faber & Faber, London,

1991: 179. Subsequent quotations are indicated by page numbers of this edition.

15. See for example, Ibn Warraq (ed.), *What the Koran Really Says: Language, Text and Commentary*, Prometheus Books, New York, 2002.

16. William Dalrymple, 'Inside the Madrasas', *New York Review of Books*, 1 December 2005, pp. 16–20.

17. Barbara Daly Metcalf, *Islamic Revival in British India: Deoband 1860–1900*, Oxford University Press, Delhi, 2005.

18. On Jinnah, see Ayaesha Jalal, *The Sole Spokesman: Jinnah, the Muslim League and the Demand for Pakistan*, Cambridge University Press-Cambridge, 1985.

19. Jason Burke, *Al-Qaeda*, I.B. Tauris, London, 2003.

20. I have discussed these matters in greater detail in *Marx's Revenge*.

21. Entry on *Ideology*, Encyclopaedia Britannica, Macropedia, pp. 768–72.

22. See my *Marx's Revenge*, chapters 4 and 5, for an outline the economic theory of Marx.

23. See Courtois et al., *The Black Book of Communism*; François Furet, *The Passing of an Illusion: The Idea of Communism in the Twentieth Century*, University of Chicago Press, Chicago, 1999.

24. Pierre-Joseph Proudhon, quoted in Marshall, *Demanding the Impossible*.

25. For an informative article on anarchism, see 'For *Jihadist*, Read Anarchist', *The Economist*, 20 August 2005.

26. Among the many books Burke, *Al Qaeda*, is the one I have found most useful.

27. For some discussion see Meghnad Desai and Yahya Said (eds), *Financial Crises and Global Governance*, Routledge, London, 2003.

28. Voting in IMF and the World Bank is weighted by the initial contributions of the members and the USA has the highest weightage in the vote. There is a lot of evidence that the USA has used the IMF and the World Bank as a tool of its foreign policy.

29. Osama Bin Laden's life is well covered in Burke, *Al-Qaeda*, and in Jonathan Randal, *Osama: The Making of a Terrorist*, Vintage Books, New York, 2005.

30. Peter Bergen confirms this non-involvement with America, in his *Holy War Inc.: Inside the Secret World of Osama bin Laden*, Free Press,

New York, 2002, p. 67.

31. The best source for Osma Bin Laden's speeches is *Messages to the World: The Statements of Osama Bin Laden*, ed. Bruce Lawrence, trans. James Howarth, Verso, London, 2005. Subsequent references to this book will be cited as with the date of the statement and the appropriate page numbers.

32. A succinct analysis of the Iranian revolution can be found in 'Iranian Revolution in Comparative Perspective', in Halliday, *Islam and the Myth of Confrontation.*

33. Patricia Crone and Martin Hinds argue that for some time after his death Muhammad was referred as just one among all the other prophets by his followers. But after a generation or so, he was given the exalted status and put as the greatest of prophets with a capital P. *God's Caliph*, ch. 3.

34. See Albert Hourani, *A History of the Arab Peoples* (Faber & Faber, London, 1991), for an account.

35. I have discussed this in my Maulana Azad Lecture, 'Globalisation and Culture', Indian Council of Cultural Relations, Delhi, 2004.

36. The literature is very large here. See among others, Peter Linnebaugh and Marcus Rediker, *The Many-Headed Hydra: Sailors, Slaves, Commoners and the Hidden History of the Revolutionary Atlantic*, Verso, London, 2000.

37. For a short introduction to what is a very large and complex literature, see the entries by Ernest Gellner on *Nation* and *Nationalism* in William Outhwaite (ed.), *The Blackwell Dictionary of Modern Social Thought*, Blackwell, Oxford, 2003.

38. See Meghnad Desai, *Development and Nationhood: Essays on the Political Economy of South Asia*, Oxford University Press, Delhi, 2005, for discussion of national problems in South Asia.

39. Avi Shlaim, *The Iron Wall: Israel and the Arab World*, Penguin, London, 2000, p. 3. Subsequent quotes from the book will be cited by page number.

40. David Cole, *Are We Safer?*, review of Daniel Benjamin and Steven Simon, *The Next Attack: The Failure of the War on Terror and a Strategy Getting It Right* (Times Books, New York, 2006), in *New York Review of Books*, 9 March 2006, pp. 15–18; p. 17.

41. Many books have come out favouring the aggressive pursuit of the

war on terror. See among others, George Friedman, *America's Secret War*, Doubleday, New York, 2004; Anonymous, *Imperial Hubris: Why the West is Losing the War on Terror*, Brassey's, New York, 2004; Steven Emerson, *American Jihad: The Terrorists Living Among Us*, Free Press, New York, 2003.

42. Ayoub *The Crisis of Muslim History*.

43. This cultural battle is well described in Frances Stonor Saunders, *Who Paid the Piper? The CIA and the Cultural Cold War*, Granta, London, 1999.

44. I have discussed this in greater detail in *Marx's Revenge*.

45. See for a recent account John Esposito and John Voll, *Makers of Contemporary Islam*, Oxford University Press, New York, 2001.

46. See Ibn Warraq (ed.), *What the Koran Really Says*.

47. There is the apocryphal story of the Texas matron who was asked if she favoured the teaching of Spanish as well as English in Texas schools and replied, 'No; if English was good enough for Jesus, it should be good enough for everybody else.'

References

Anonymous (2004) *Imperial Hubris: Why the West is Losing the War on Terror* (New York: Brassey's).

Ayoub, Mahmoud (2003) *The Crisis of Muslim History: Religion and Politics in Early Islam* (Oxford: One World).

Bergen, Peter (2002) *Holy War, Inc.: Inside the Secret World of Osama bin Laden* (New York: Free Press).

Benjamin, Daniel, and Steven Simon (2006) *The Next Attack: The Failure of the War on Terror and a Strategy for Getting It Right* (New York: Times Books).

Burke, Jason (2003) *Al-Qaeda* (London: I.B. Tauris).

Chang, Jung, and Jon Halliday (2005) *Mao* (London: Cape).

Cole, David (2006) 'Are We Safer?', *New York Review of Books*, 9 March.

Courtois, Stephane, et al., *The Black Book of Communism* (Cambridge, MA: Harvard University Press).

Crone, Patricia, and Martin Hinds (1986) *God's Caliph* (Cambridge: Cambridge University Press).

Dalrymple, W. (2005) 'Inside the Madrasas', *New York Review of Books*, 1 December.

Desai, Meghnad (2002) *Marx's Revenge: The Resurgence of Capitalism and the Death of Statist Socialism* (London: Verso).

———— (2004) 'Globalisation and Culture: The Maulana Azad Lecture', Delhi, 14 December (Delhi: Indian Council for Cultural Relations).

———— (2005) *Development and Nationhood: Essays in the Political Economy of South Asia* (Delhi: Oxford University Press).

———— (2005) Letter to *The Financial Times*, 10 August.

Desai, Meghnad, and Yahya Said (eds) (2003) *Global Governance and Financial Crises* (London: Routledge).

The Economist (2005) 'For *Jihadist*, Read Anarchist', 20 August.

Emerson, Steven (2002) *American Jihad: The Terrorists Living among Us* (New York: Free Press).

Encyclopaedia Britannica, entry on 'Ideology', Macropedia.

Esposito, James and John Voll (2001) *Makers of Contemporary Islam* (New York: Oxford University Press).

Friedman, George (2004) *America's Secret War: Inside the Worldwide Struggle Between America and Its Enemies* (New York: Broadways Books).

Furet, François (1999) *The Passing of an Illusion: The Idea of Communism in the Twentieth Century* (Chicago: University of Chicago Press).

Gellner, Ernest (2003) Entries on 'Nation' and 'Nationalism', in Outhwaite, *Blackwell Dictionary of Modern Social Thought*.

Halliday, Fred (1996) *Islam and the Myth of Confrontation: Religion and Politics in the Middle East* (London: I.B. Tauris).

Hourani, Albert (1991) *A History of the Arab Peoples* (London: Faber & Faber).

Huntington, Samuel (1993) 'The Clash of Civilizations?', *Foreign Affairs*, Summer.

———— (1996) *The Clash of Civilizations and the Remaking of World Order* (New York: Simon & Schuster).

Iqbal, Muhammad (1981) *Shikwa and Jawab-e-Shikwa: Iqbal's Dialogue with Allah*, trans. and introduced by Khushwant Singh (Delhi: Oxford University Press).

Jalal, Ayesha (1985) *The Sole Spokesman: Jinnah, the Muslim League and the Demand for Pakistan* (Cambridge: Cambridge University Press) .

Laden, Osama Bin (2005) *Messages to the World: The Statements of Osama Bin Laden*, edited and introduced by Bruce Lawrence, trans. James Howarth (London: Verso).

Linebaugh, Peter and Marcus Rediker (2000) *The Many-Headed Hydra: Sailors, Slaves, Commoners and the Hidden History of the Revolutionary Atlantic* (London: Verso).

Mackay, Ruddock (1985) *Balfour: Intellectual Statesman* (Oxford: Oxford University Press).

Manji, Irshad (2005) *The Trouble with Islam Today: A Wake up Call for Honesty and Change* (London: Mainstream Publishing).

Marshall, Peter (1992) *Demanding the Impossible: A History of Anarchism* (London: HarperCollins).

Metcalfe, Barbara Daly (2002) *Islamic Revival in British India: Deoband 1860–1900*, 2nd edn (Delhi: Oxford University Press).

Outhwaite, William (ed.) (2003) *The Blackwell Dictionary of Modern Social Thought*, 2nd edn, (Oxford: Basil Blackwell).

Randall, Jonathan (2004) *Osama: The Making of a Terrorist* (New York: Vintage).

Roy, Olivier (1994) *The Failure of Political Islam* (Cambridge MA: Harvard Univrsity Press).

———(2005) *Globalised Islam: The Search for a New Ummah* (London: C. Hurst).

Sen, Amartya (2005) *The Argumentative Indian: Writings on Indian History, Culture and Identity* (London: Allen Lane).

Shlaim, Avi (2000) *The Iron Wall: Israel and the Arab World* (Penguin; London).

Warraq, Ibn (2002) *What the Koran Rally Says: Language, Text and Commentary* (Amherst NY: Prometheus Books).

Index